STEPPING OUT
Your Strategic Playbook
for Launching as an
Emerging Entrepreneur

About Kimberly Pitts, UImpact, LLC

Kimberly Pitts is the proud founder of UImpact, LLC. Uimpact is a *Branding and Marketing* company, dedicated to helping entrepreneurial women learn and apply branding and marketing strategies to position their businesses in the market, attract their target audiences, create influential brands, realize more income, and enjoy freedom in both their businesses and their lives. We do this through our premier training-based mastermind program-*Thrive Academy*, our *Branding VIP Program*, our *Packaged for Growth Annual Conference*, and a myriad of ongoing training programs.

Anything but conventional, our creative and innovative techniques will challenge you, encourage you, inspire you, and equip you to get to the place you desire, and deserve to be.

Our mission and purpose is to empower and encourage entrepreneurial women to courageously step outside of the box and build towards what they know they are purposed to do. We advocate healthy businesses, healthy relationships, and healthy lives when building sustainable businesses.

Whether you are in the start-up stages of your business or you're ready to grow to the next level of success and expand your reach, we are here to provide expert coaching and mentoring to better position you and your business for greater influence.

If you would like to learn more about us and what we have designed for you, please visit us at UImpact.net.

STEPPING OUT
Your Strategic Playbook
for Launching as an
Emerging Entrepreneur

Compiled by Kimberly Pitts

Co-authored by:

Latonia Bosley
Andrea Sullenger
Tonya Thomas
Angela Warr
Claudia Rodriguez
Dondra Bassett
Gabrielle Smith
Kimberly Pitts

Splendor Publishing
College Station, TX

SPLENDOR PUBLISHING
Published by Splendor Publishing
College Station, TX.

First published printing, September, 2014

Library of Congress Control Number: 2014950654
Stepping Out:
Your Strategic Playbook for Launching as an Emerging Entrepreneur
1. Business 2. Internet

ISBN-10:1940278163
ISBN-13:978-1-940278-16-2
Business/Internet

Printed in the United States of America.

Cover Background: 27881995 Yeyendesign | Dreamstime
Cover Design: Copyright © Splendor Publishing
Interior Design and Layout: Splendor Publishing
For more information, or to order bulk copies of this book for events or training, please contact SplendorPublishing.com.

Dedication

"Every time you state what you want or believe, you're the first to hear it. It's a message to both you and others about what you think is possible. Don't put a ceiling on yourself."

- Oprah Winfrey

To the many inspired, committed, and focused entrepreneurs who have a vision, message, and a clear purpose—this book is dedicated to you. The pages were written with you in mind to provide you new perspectives, new approaches, and new ways of looking at how you can continue on your entrepreneurial journey.

Thank you to the authors in this book who shared from your heart your experience and your perspective from where you are today. Without your words on these pages, many would not know the blessing it is to be an entrepreneur.

Contents

A Word from Kimberly Pitts

"*If you build it, they will come.*" If only this statement was true! When I started my business this was the truth that I truly lived by. I thought if I worked those long hours, made all the right connections, and had the best looking website, then clients would beat down my door. Does that sound familiar?

Sadly, so many entrepreneurs operate their business with this mindset. This mindset kept me locked into frustration, lack, and feeling like I was always doing something wrong; it kept me locked in a place of not growing. I had to make a decision that what I believed to be true, was not *truth*. If I build it, I need to create the right structure for my ideal clients to come.

If you are one of those entrepreneurs who has operated from, "*If you build it, they will come,*" then you are probably not doing the following:

- Consistently marketing your business every day

- Actively networking where your ideal clients hang out

- Consistently bringing in new clients

- Creating systems to help build a firm foundation for your business

One of the biggest misconceptions of entrepreneurs is that if you have a great service or product, you don't need to do any real marketing because your ideal client will want your service and/or product.

The hard reality is that you have to spend time on developing systems, setting up your business the right way, creating a branding outline, mapping out your marketing activities, and investing in your growth. So how do you do this when you have a thousand other things to do such as returning calls, sending/answering emails, attending networking events, creating proposals, etc . . . ? That is what this book will address for you. We have eight successful authors who will outline key areas they mastered when they were an emerging entrepreneur.

Here's To Your Success!

Kimberly

Chapter 1

Investing in Yourself
by Latonia Bosley

*O*ne of the most challenging things to do in life is investing in yourself and your dreams; however, it is one of the best investments you can ever make. As a new entrepreneur, it is essential that you invest in yourself. The entrepreneur's business will only grow as much as the entrepreneur grows and self-develops. I would like to share with you some information and a few action steps that were instrumental in my business that could assist you in "Launching as an Emerging Entrepreneur."

The most powerful word in the English language other than to state your name is to say the pronoun "I." Business has been shaped throughout history by men and women who established their own mantra and who were unafraid to challenge conventional wisdom. New markets, new clients, and a new way of conducting business are the byproduct of applying "I" to what stands in front of you. What Bill Gates and Paul Allen did with Microsoft was to build upon the norm and then take the idea of software in an entirely different direction.

Sam Walton repackaged the concept of how you present known merchandise to the public. His ideas were not about identifying products or brand loyalty, he left that to others. He instead fostered the proposition that a product can be made to be viewed in an entirely different manner through price reduction and marketing.

Are these deep and philosophical strands of thoughts? No. Yet Sears and Kmart were oblivious to what was transpiring. Vision, intuition, and a willingness to take risks are the hallmarks of the consummate entrepreneur who causes revolutions in thinking, execution of processes, and thus altering the end result. Entrepreneurs are leaders. They, along with scientists, explorers, inventors, educators, and writers have inspired mankind and elevated its thinking. You cannot be a consummate entrepreneur who changes and shifts the direction of what has been the norm while being a passive thinker; we must be Socrates wearing a business suit. It does not matter if you refuse to be shackled to what others are doing. What is most relevant is how "I," in this case *you*, assume the challenge and conquer it. Ideas hatched by entrepreneurs are meant to change the world and continuously alter the established business model. Hans F. Hansen stated, "*It takes nothing to join the crowd. It takes everything to stand alone.*" Be an independent thinker, examine the norm at every opportunity, and then make it better. Invest in yourself as the wise poker player does. Know when to up the ante and also when to pull back. Combine the words "I" and investment.

As a new entrepreneur, I found that in order for me to be successful in my business, I needed to take a few steps to position myself for success by *investing* in myself. I did this by increasing and developing my skills, knowledge, and education, seeking the assistance of a mentor/business coach, and increasing my professional and personal networking circles.

Everyone possesses certain skills and a level of knowledge or experience that can be improved upon and utilized to start a successful business. I once read that investing in human capital leads to entrepreneurs. Human capital is defined as an individual's knowledge, skills, and abilities, which are the key characteristics of entrepreneurs.

Knowledge is the substance that must be acquired by the entrepreneur through every means possible. Volumes of information are available through webinars, teleseminars, CDs, DVDs, and from a variety of other sources. What is also invaluable is to read about how great men and women from previous eras, as well as from today, have successfully navigated through the process of entrepreneurship. Despite not being an entrepreneur, Warren Buffett is a sage on how to acquire wealth, nurture it, and select a winning team. A company or business is no better than the individuals leading it. This is a return to the themes of critical thinking, practical skills, and interpersonal skills.

Improving your human capital which consists of your skills or knowledge is a wise investment to better position yourself to advance in your current career, transition into a new career path, or to become an entrepreneur. Successful entrepreneurs seek to improve in their interpersonal, critical thinking, and practical skills.

Interpersonal skills consist of leadership, communication, and negotiation. You use your interpersonal skills on a daily basis when you interact and communicate with people.

Entrepreneurs who have spent time developing strong interpersonal skills tend to be more successful in their business. Are you a leader? Are you able to motivate or lead others to believe in your business' mission or values and to carry out the mission? As a leader, it is important to know your strengths, weaknesses, and leadership style so you will know how to effectively lead your team and run your business. You will need to develop this skill to be able to delegate responsibilities with the confidence that your business can run without you being present.

John F. Kennedy stated, "*Leadership and learning are indispensable to each other.*" Take a leadership assessment to determine your leadership style, and then spend some time researching how to effectively lead others with your leadership style. I recommend reading *The Leadership Challenge*, by James Kouzes and Barry Posner. This book provides research-based leadership strategies and five practices of exemplary leadership.

Communication is another very important skill to have in life. We usually spend the majority of our waking hours communicating in some form with others. To grow your company, you must be able to successfully communicate your purpose and game plan for the business. As an entrepreneur, it is extremely important that you are able to communicate and build relationships with people. You will develop relationships with potential clients or customers, potential investors, other businesses and organizations, suppliers, and most importantly, your employees, staff, or team. To be successful, you will have to depend on others to assist you in the early stage of your business, and trust me, it is too much for you to tackle on your own.

You should learn about the different barriers to good communication so you will be aware of the pitfalls of ineffective communication. Conveying a clear and concise message involves overcoming these barriers through active listening, seeking clarification, and reflection on what has been communicated.

Successful entrepreneurs frequently speak in the abstract when initially sharing an idea with a fellow entrepreneur, colleague, or a staff member. World-class politicians, diplomats, and thinkers also do the same in energizing an audience. Sir Richard Branson of the Virgin Group, Larry Page and Sergey Brin—the co-founders of Google, and noted American inventor Thomas Edison, have or had the ability to enable individuals to journey inside their minds as they discussed ideas and concepts. Thus, we find that outstanding communication skills are necessary for professional growth and the evolving of concepts and intangible products.

Both success and failure start at the top; you can do anything on paper. The trick is being able to enlist the various skills of the staff in a harmonious manner that delivers what has been visualized in your mind. Philosophers and educators would both describe communication as nothing more than the transfer of information or data from one person to another.

It is also important that an entrepreneur possess the ability to listen, because it serves as the foundation for learning new business concepts that will help you build your business. What education or training have you invested in that enables you to listen so that you really understand another person from their frame of reference? Very few people have had any type of training on listening. Good communication should be efficient and effective. If you want to interact effectively with me and influence me to work with you, you need to first listen and understand me. *"Seek first to understand"* involves a shift in the way we believe communication to be. The majority of people do not listen with the intent of understanding others; they tend to listen with the intent to form a response.

If you want to be a skilled communicator, you need to be effective in all areas in the communication process and you must be comfortable communicating through all entry points into your business, such as face-to-face, written, and through technology. Social media is a powerful tool in business, and it will prove beneficial for you to effectively utilize this tool to communicate with your market. There are many ways to use social media to communicate with your potential customers or clients. Entrepreneurs are using social media through Twitter, LinkedIn, Facebook, Instagram, podcasts, and blogs, to name a few. You should spend time researching these options to determine the best way for you to connect with your customers or clients.

Once you improve your communication skills, another vital skill an entrepreneur must learn or possess is the ability to negotiate competently. Poor negotiation skills could be detrimental in your business by causing you to lose a lot of customers and money. You not only need to be able to negotiate your fees or prices and agreements with potential customers, you will also need to be able to negotiate differences between people in a mutually favorable way. A few tips to effectively negotiate is to not be intimidated, be prepared by knowing your objective and what you want to see as an outcome, listen, and be prepared to walk away. The success of your business lies with you and your ability to effectively negotiate. An admirable principle for an entrepreneur to follow is one of the basic tenets of President Theodore Roosevelt. He would often ask himself what he would do if he were in the other person's position in the negotiations or talks that were transpiring. Life coaches and business gurus would agree with this practice.

Changing places with the other person enables you to view the conversation through their eyes. Now you have two ways to look at the idea being discussed. This also prepares you to understand exactly what the other person is seeking. Look for the four-way premise in these negotiations. Good for me, good for them, good for the business, and good for the public.

Individuals prefer doing business with those who are concerned about the outcome for all parties.

Entrepreneurs tend to be a bit creative and innovative; however, if you are not very creative, don't worry because creativity is a skill that can be developed if you will invest the time and effort. Being able to critically see your ideas before acting upon your creativity allows you to consider all of your options and possibly save you a lot of time and money. Critical thinking takes a lot of discipline. It is not just about "thinking," it is about "thinking better." Using your critical thinking skills involves seeking information, analyzing the information, and logical reasoning. There are a few strategies you could explore to help you improve your critical thinking skills. Ask questions to get a clear understanding, assemble all relevant information, and keep an open mind by thinking outside the box. Some people would even recommend getting *rid* of the box. When you go through this process, it allows you to make the best decision possible for your business. Critical thinking is a characteristic of growth and can benefit you as an entrepreneur in your decision-making process.

To effectively run your business, you need practical skills such as goal setting, organizational, and management skills. With entrepreneurs running the day-to-day business, scheduling business-building activities, and seeking new business opportunities, it is easy to lose sight of the vision of your company. One thing that successful entrepreneurs have in common is their ability to set, initiate, and complete their goals. What are your business goals? Do you want to increase your client base? Do you want to increase your business revenue? Where do you see your business in five years? Research shows when entrepreneurs set measurable goals for themselves, they are more likely to achieve their goals. Setting goals allows you to use your short-term motivation to achieve your long-term vision. Setting goals also focuses on your attainment of knowledge and helps you organize your time, finances, human capital, and other resources to successfully build your business. By setting clearly defined goals, you can measure the achievement of your goals and you will be able to see forward progress in reaching your dream of a thriving and successful business. Your confidence level is also increased as you recognize your ability in achieving the goals you have set. Setting goals involves a reasonable amount of reflection into what is working in your business and where you want to see your business in the future.

There are several methods to set business or company goals. You can research different methods to see what works best for you; however, I like to keep it simple. I use the SMART method, which is:

- **S**—Specific

- **M**—Measurable

- **A**—Achievable

- **R**—Realistic

- **T**—Timely

If your goal this year is to increase your customers or your client base, instead of saying "*I want to have more customers this year,*" you need to be more specific and say, "*I want to increase my customer or client base by _____*" (a realistic percentage or amount). You should be able to measure your progress towards your goals. You could track your progress in several ways: weekly, monthly, or quarterly, in comparison to the previous year. When setting your timeline for achieving your goals, make sure you are realistic. Instead of shooting for the long-term goals, break them down into smaller achievable goals, which in turn give you measurable, attainable, and short-term goals for which to strive. Create a roadmap of success by typing your business goals and the action you will take to achieve them. It would be a good idea to display them on a board where you can review them on a regular basis and track your achievements.

Organizational skills are also important for entrepreneurs. Running a business will require you to juggle many tasks at any given time. You may have a business meeting across town, a request for a business quote, delivery of merchandise to a client or customer, and you may need to prepare for an upcoming event. If you do not have a task management or time management system in place, you are setting yourself up for failure and undue stress. Running your business without these types of systems in place will cause you to be unproductive in your day-to-day business tasks. Using some type of planner shifts you from just doing your business to growing your business by keeping you focused on essential activities to move your business forward.

There are many planners and organizers from which to choose. You can invest hundreds of dollars for a complete system or you can download free guides and templates from the Internet.

Management skills are definitely important in running a business. If you are going to be a successful entrepreneur, you must develop a level of expertise in managing people, money, operations, sales, marketing, and your overall business affairs. The key to managing several activities in your business is the ability to delegate along with good time management. Focus on your level of expertise and hire someone or a staff to handle what you are not good at doing. An indication of good management skills is to outsource what you cannot do, and create and implement good systems and processes to run your business. This will allow you to spend more time on business-building activities such as developing new services, creating new products, building new client relationships, and increasing revenue. Making the time you are currently investing in your business twice as productive is the key to its success.

Now that you have this information, asses your skills and begin investing time to improve upon them. The harder you work to improve your skills both personal and professional, the more successful you will be.

> *"You must either modify your dreams or magnify your skills"* -Jim Rohn

I believe that entrepreneurs can increase their chances of success by investing in their knowledge. There are many ways to invest in increasing your knowledge, and the least expensive way would be to just pick up a book with information that interest you. There are countless books, blogs, news articles, and magazines that provide information on nearly any topic imaginable. Search and research topics on the Internet that relate to the skills you want to improve upon, and keep up to date with the latest advancements or trends in your area of interest.

Expanding your knowledge and skills does not have to be limited to your business or profession. It can also include improving your knowledge about a personal passion. For example, if you are interested in baking, you could search the Internet for countless recipes or attend cooking classes.

The knowledge and skills you gain from cooking classes could open an opportunity to start a baking business. I am a firm believer that by pursuing your passion and what you are interested in, you can effectively invest in yourself.

In addition to searching the Internet and reading books that peak your interest, it would also be beneficial to search articles or publications and read books on personal and professional development. As an entrepreneur, investing in your personal development is just as important as investing in your professional development because as you grow personally, you will grow professionally. Many entrepreneurs spend so much time on developing and growing their business that they do not realize how important their personal development is to the success of their business. Developing your personal goals puts things in perspective and helps create an action plan that makes your goals more achievable. A personal or professional goal could be to increase your income; however to reach this goal, an action plan must be created to track progress or success. Find books or material that will guide you in creating action plans for your business. Harry Truman said, "*All leaders are readers.*" There is a great wealth of knowledge to gain from others' experiences through books, blogs, articles, and publications. I have always maintained a rule to invest at least five percent of my income in my personal development. As I continue to grow, so does my business and my income.

Benjamin Franklin stated, "*If a man empties his purse into his head, no one can take it away from him. An investment in knowledge always pays the best interest.*" I truly believe that sacrificing and investing in your education and increasing your knowledge is extremely important because the more you know, the more powerful you are. You will be in a better position to increase your earning potential in your career or business, provide for yourself and your family, and create greater opportunities in your life.

With the options of financial aid, scholarships, grants, and taking classes online or in person, there should be no excuse. There is no reason not to take advantage of investing in your education.

After being employed for over eight years with a company, my position was eliminated and I was laid off with no plan

"B" to fall back on. I was left trying to figure out what my next move was going to be and how I was going to be able to provide for my children with no income, resources, or family support. Through fear, frustration, and loss of employment, I made the conscious decision that I was going to do what was necessary to invest in myself by obtaining a degree to increase my knowledge, skills, and earning potential. After countless hours of searching for employment, I found a full-time job and a part-time job, and managed to put myself through college and obtained an Associate, Bachelor, and Master's degree. During the time pursuing my degrees, I also put one of my children through college and realized my dream of becoming an entrepreneur. Now that I have my degrees in a field I am passionate about, I am able to transfer the skills and knowledge I obtained in class to my business. This was also a part of my personal development. I had to sacrifice a lot of time with my children to work on classwork and business-building activities; however, these experiences have taught me a valuable life lesson on how important it is to increase my knowledge and skills by sacrificing and investing in myself.

Taking advantage of additional training is another way to invest in your knowledge and skills. This training can be in the form of conferences, e-courses, telesummits, webinars, and workshops. These trainings are usually low in cost, yet they provide a wealth of information and tools to utilize in your business and daily life. Businesses usually offer workshops to their employees at no charge and may pay for additional outside training.

As a new entrepreneur, I knew I needed to position myself with a solid foundation for my business. I needed to gain more knowledge in marketing, branding, and building a business.

Attending a "Packaged for Growth" conference presented by Kimberly Pitts with UImpact was one of the best investments I have made in my life. The wealth of information, knowledge, and tools I received from the conference changed my life and provided me with the information I needed to launch my business.

Attending business conferences provides many benefits to entrepreneurs. You will have an opportunity to interact and hear what other entrepreneurs are doing in their businesses. This may get your creative juices going to see what you can do differently in your business.

On that same note, attending business conferences will allow you to see and get to know your competitors' strengths and weaknesses, and provide you with information on what you can do to increase your competitive edge. One of the main benefits of attending a business conference is to hear from the experts and learn something new. When you attend a conference, you have access to the experts to ask questions, share ideas, and expand on what was covered. These informal relations that take place are invaluable, and you should never pass up the opportunity to interact with the experts.

My attendance at the conference made me realize I needed ongoing support in building my business, so I secured a business coach/mentor. To find mentors, you have to seek out people in your business and follow their example. I was taught to find an expert and do *exactly* what they tell you to do. People who have been successful in their business love to tell their story. So in the beginning I would ask for a consultation, a thirty-minute lunch, or a fifteen-minute phone conversation to learn how they built a successful business. For a new entrepreneur, hiring a business coach is a wise investment. Regardless of where your business is, there is always room for improvement. A good business coach will provide support in building your business because they have gained the experience in setting up a business, marketing, branding, website design, and networking. They have pretty much done all of the groundwork and drafted a blueprint for success. A business coach will meet with you to get an understanding of where you are in your business and your vision for the business. You will write down your business goals and create the plan to make it happen. You will then put down the forecasts for revenue, costs, and profits, which means you can track the progress of your business. This also helps you make adjustments in a timely manner if the plan needs to be improved. You will create systems that will become the basis of a manual designed to describe how the business works day by day, week by week, and eliminate the frustrations by which new entrepreneurs can often be overwhelmed. Your coach will help you make a plan, keep you on track, hold you accountable, and expect results because you have been provided with the tools necessary to achieve results. Ultimately, your business coach's job is to arm you with the tools and knowledge that will help you to become successful.

When you decide to hire a business coach/mentor, do extensive research to ensure you are hiring the best person to help you grow your business. I believe hiring a good business coach/mentor is one of the best investments you can make to ensure the success of your business.

Networking is important, and attending business conferences give you access to other conference attendees, which is an excellent time to make connections, share information, and learn about other businesses. Making connections makes good business sense because you never know when you might want to team up for a joint-venture or make a referral to someone you met at a conference. Networking is also a way to build relationships and generate referrals for your business. There are several ways to network. Attending conferences was one way to network; attending a "meet up" is another way to network. Meetup is one of the largest networks of local groups. You can search areas of interests and find a Meetup group to join. Usually there is a small fee involved; however, the networking opportunity could be beneficial.

Using LinkedIn is another great way to make new business connections and build credibility to assist in growing your business. To network on LinkedIn, you will need to search for groups that interest you and join those groups. You can search by geographical location, business type, industry, and even by business name. Once you join a group, you can begin to interact with the members in a group setting, or you can send private messages. Corporations are creating groups on LinkedIn as well. Corporate groups consist of corporations that have partnered with other corporations or brands to help build larger groups. Again, this is a great opportunity to join a large professional network and meet other business people and entrepreneurs. Joining your local Chamber of Commerce offers many networking opportunities. The Chamber of Commerce allows business owners to keep abreast of important trends and current issues in their community and local market. A research study revealed that when consumers know that a business is a member of their local chamber of commerce, they are forty percent more likely to think favorably of it and sixty-three percent more likely to purchase goods or services from the business in the future.

Serving on chamber committees opens up numerous networking opportunities and can also help you promote your professional skills. Membership has its privileges! New members are listed in all of the chamber's correspondence including their publication, newsletter, and certain Facebook information. Membership with the chamber also opens up an opportunity for them to promote your company's grand opening with a ribbon cutting ceremony. This allows for a great opportunity for people to see and inquire about your business that could lead to potential clients and increased revenue.

As I previously mentioned, one of the most challenging things to do in life is to invest in yourself and your dream of becoming an entrepreneur. As a single mother and entrepreneur, I have spent the majority of my time trying to figure out how I was going to maintain my household, provide for my family, and build my business. I spent my life focusing and investing all of my time and finances on everyone else, and never took the time to invest in myself. As women and mothers, we at times create environments around ourselves to support why we *can't* invest in ourselves. There is never enough time in a day to work a full-time job, clean the house, pay the bills, and spend quality time with the family while building a business.

Our finances and time are usually stretched beyond our means and it is difficult to choose where to invest our energy and time. We have all been faced with life's challenges where we've had to make difficult decisions, and make sacrifices that can have a lasting effect on our self and our family. Through it all, we must realize the importance of taking the time to invest in ourselves, our dreams and our businesses to "Launch as an Emerging Entrepreneur."

About Latonia Bosley

Latonia S. Bosley is the founder of "Next Level Moms." Her purpose in life is to support moms who are ready to find their purpose, plan their move, and position themselves to transition to the next level in life. She has worked in higher education for over thirteen years, has a Master's degree in Healthcare Administration, and is a lifetime member of the Alpha Chi National College Honor Society.

Learn More Here:
NextLevelMoms.com

Continue the Conversation on . . .

Facebook: Facebook.com/latonia.bosley

Chapter 2

Emerging with Influence
by Andrea Sullenger

$\mathcal{J}$t's "Decision Time!" Creating your dream entrepreneurial experience is predicated on you establishing your own unique entrepreneur identity. It is about you laying claim to how you want to be seen and heard, how you want to serve the world, and what makes you different from all the others. Let's begin with eight questions that will help you identify who you are and how you are going to show up as you create your dream business.

1. Start with WHY. *Why* do you want to be an entrepreneur? Do you know? Have you ever written it out? If not, I would strongly suggest you do, and that you come up with at least a hundred reasons why you want this. Entrepreneurship isn't easy and if you can't come up with a rock-solid list of why you are choosing it, you will bail when you turn a corner and see another mountain to climb. I would also suggest you read the book, *Start With Why*, by Simon Sinek. It is a great read and a *must* for all entrepreneurs.

2. What strengths and unique gifts do you believe you are bringing to the entrepreneurial playground?

3. Are these strengths different from others out there and if so, how?

4. Who do you want to serve and bring value to? This is your target market. For example, lawyers, dry cleaner owners, or salon owners.

5. Who is your niche? This is the laser focused and drilled down group within your target market you wish to work with. For example, female lawyers, brand new salon owners, established dry cleaner owners with yearly revenue of at least $200,000 or who have been in business for a minimum of five years.

6. What type of service, product, or programs do you want to offer this group?

7. How do you wish to accomplish delivering of these services, products, or programs?

8. Do you know how to create these products and deliver them? If not, what will you need to learn to make this happen?

Positioning is all about choosing how you become seen and known to your perfect audience and your networking partners. It is the deployment of you placing yourself into perfect visibility to create the business you desire. Building the right positioning for yourself isn't about doing business as usual or about following the rules.

If you want to create high impact positioning, you have to decide that you will be the one to write your own rules. You be the author of your path. People are desperate to see, relate, and follow someone that can do exactly that. When you write your own rules and carve out your sweet spot, you create engagement, a following, and a confidence others will have for you and your work. Positioning isn't something you can purchase from an online program, a book, a workshop, a certification, or degree. Positioning comes from you choosing it, going after it, and claiming it until your work and name are so big and impactful that you no longer need to introduce yourself.

How will you know if the target market and your initial niche are a perfect match right out of the gate? Chances are, you won't. Chances are as you grow the business and yourself, your understanding and knowledge will evolve. As you grow, your focus and attention will become tightened. Most entrepreneurs are held captive in the beginning from fear of selecting the wrong target market, the wrong niche, and not being able to deliver high quality service, so they cast the net wide. They are so afraid of excluding someone or some group that they want to include everyone. The reality is, you can't be profound and effective by working with or serving everyone. Your message becomes lost. The best way for you to *not* get stuck in the crevasse of fear and avoid *not* claiming your place in a market is to simply decide what you want. Write it out. You don't have to have all of the answers right this moment, you just have to choose to begin. After you have chosen, you can spend some intentional time researching the details and laying the foundation for what your target market and niche will really shake out to be. One word of caution here, don't allow your inner censor to squash your vision. Your seedling ideas may not work out completely how you have pictured them but they are most likely extending from an inner connectedness. They are most likely bubbling to the surface because they call to who you really are, who you really enjoy working and being with, and to your innate skills, gifts, and talents. The inner censor will tell you things like, *"No one has ever done that before so chances are it won't work"* or, *"Is that really acceptable?"* or, *"What makes you think you could add value to that group of people?"* . . . and so much more. Silence the inner censor (which we all have). Tell her to shut up, and then continue to immerse yourself in the choosing of who you are and how you will serve the world. Take the next step and do your homework. Research eight to ten entrepreneurs that cater to your ideal target market. What value do they bring to them? What is the niche they possess? Take a look at the language they use on their website, social media, and any marketing collateral. Through the written words they use you may be able to identify details about the target market you missed, their core challenge and need, and the transformation that they can expect to gain by working with that company and entrepreneur. This exercise isn't meant for you to fall prey to copying what others in the same or similar market are doing. Nor is it a shot for you to beat yourself up about how much farther they are down the rabbit trail than you. This is simply research, idea-stimulating research.

New entrepreneurs are coming onto the scene all the time, literally daily. Some come in and go out in the same day while others create massive waves and build ridiculously amazing followings. Why? Aren't we all faced with the task of sculpting our uniqueness and rising above the noise and competition? Truth is, we are. So why is it that some make it and others don't? I think it simple really, I think some actually believe they've now entered some competitive race, and when they see it's a marathon and not a sprint, or that hundreds who started sooner are ahead of them, they bail. If some can come in "late" and craft successful businesses with massive impact, then it only proves there is no competition outside of oneself. The confrontation we face is the discovery of what makes us unique. What sets you apart from others inside of the same target market? Clarity is power, so let's get clear about your unique gifts and talents. Take out a sheet of paper and write down as many things as you can think of at which you are really great—things you do well. These things don't have to be solely geared towards the entrepreneurial endeavor to which you are adventuring. Next, list the things that excite your soul and you absolutely love doing.

Now ask twenty-five friends to tell you the things they believe are your greatest strengths or talents. How do the lists meet up? Do you see some common words or phrases that keep popping up for people? How could these strengths translate into value extended and given to your ideal target market?

Remember, I said positioning isn't something that happens to you. Positioning is something you construct. Once the foundation of who you are and how you show up in the entrepreneurial wonderland, and who and how you serve is defined, then you can be confident it is time for you to do what I call, "take the stage." Have you ever been to a concert for a famous rock and roller? The concerts I have been to don't seem to have someone announcing who will be coming on stage. In my experience, the energy is high, the stadium goes dark, the music blasts, and the performers and the band burst onto the stage; lights illuminate, and they powerfully enter into their work, their first song. Sure, there is some guy back stage who says, "OK, go on now," but there is no big announcement. Why? Because we, the attendees, are in the audience waiting with anticipatory excitement to be given an incredible show. The world is also waiting for this. There are millions and millions of people out there waiting for you to storm the stage and give them a show. I am the stage manager and I am telling you, "It is time to go on!" How do you "take the stage"? You do it like a rock star, that's how. You grab hold of your unique talents, gifts, and your network, and you go give it away. I don't necessarily mean you give it away for free, but in some cases that actually will be true. It is your time to build your platform and position. There are a hundred and one ways to create visibility. The main thing is that you select two or three of them, and implement them right away. One of the things I do to set myself apart and to create authority, credibility, engagement, and visibility is to play the role of interviewer. I do an interview series where I showcase powerful, creative, and inspiring women entrepreneurs. This one stage-taking activity instantly creates connection, places me in the role of professional, and lends me the opportunity to work from a place of credibility. Come up with a list of ways you can "take the stage" and begin building your powerful positioning this week.

Birthing your best business and life isn't easy. Most of the time it isn't fast either. However, you can build the perfectly matched business and life. One that offers external and internal rewards beyond your wildest dreams if you are willing to do the work; if you are willing to get out of your own way and out of your own head where that internal censor lives. To be an extraordinary entrepreneur you have to dig deep and pull up that internal confidence, and strength, and find who you have a passion to help.

Network Your Hiney Off

In a world where doing more in less time, "faster is better," and non-stop communication through technology trumps face-to-face connection, the art of mindful and courageous engagement has become lost. It is a practice that has been pushed to the back seat, maybe even the trunk. As entrepreneurs, it is vital for us to course correct and once again adopt the practice of engaging in face-to-face or ear-to-ear relationship building. Let's get honest with one another, no entrepreneur, including me, has ever built anything of significance because we made a vision board, hung out our shingle, and the masses came running. Nope . . . none of us have had it unfold quite like that. The reality is, it takes far more than doing either one of those tasks to attract and create the idea clients—clients who perform at their peak and refer their network.

I don't know what type of business you want to have or are creating, but chances are you leverage the Internet in some capacity. That's great, but don't get sucked into the belief that you can automate it all, talk to no one, be seen by no one right out of the gate, and still be attracting and creating more clients than you can handle. The guys and gals you read about who share how they are living life to the fullest, working two hours a week with everything else automated, and still raking in a cool million each month didn't start off that way. Believe me. For some of you, working completely automated will never take place because your business is totally based on relationships and interaction. I'm a coach, so this is true for me, and if I decided I didn't want to engage with people, I would soon be living in a box. Not a pretty sight. I am all about automation and leveraging your knowledge, but when it comes to creating new clients, you will be hard pressed to yank yourself out of the mix and still maintain above average results.

Creating clients sounds harder than it is. Creating clients is simply you putting yourself out there and intentionally having the right conversations with networking partners or people who you would love as your clients. Making sure you are clear about who you serve—your target market—and knowing what you offer them is step one. Networking is critical to any entrepreneur but especially one who is just getting established or working to up-level their business. There is definitely a right way to network, a right way to build relationships, a right way to ask for what you need, and a right way to give what your networking partners need. After you identify what you need, identify who can help you. When looking into your network don't just identify those who stand out as an obvious match to supply you with your initial wants. Look at the list of people and ask yourself, who has or does something that compliments what I am after, what I do. Who is a direct competitor? To whom on this list can I offer something of value? Who on this list is powerful and who—if I had their endorsement—would propel me through to the moon and back?

The art of networking is remembering a few simple things:

1. Being a giver first always pays ten-fold. Look for ways you can offer value first before you ever even approach someone about what you want or need. A simple way to do this is to ask, *"What do you need currently; how might I bring value to you?"*

2. Be a committed listener . . . take notes . . . you won't remember it all. I promise.

3. Remember that building a strong networking partner-ship is about trust, which doesn't generally come from one conversation. It takes time and multiple conversations.

4. When you do ask or reply about what you need or want, be specific. Make it so easy, so simple for the other person to assist you, that they feel like they just hit an "easy" button and it was no big deal. Don't say things like, *"I'm just open to new clients and looking,"* rather say something like this, *"You know, I serve female*

entrepreneurs who are looking to create digital products and leverage their time. Currently, I have an opening to take on one more client. Do you know any female entrepreneurs who want to leverage their time and up their income, to whom you would be willing to introduce me? I'd love to have an introduction and initial conversation with them to see if I may be able to offer value." If they say yes or if they say no, it's okay, but the next step is to take the next step! One thing I like to do is to let them know I will email them what I am after, with a short email they could literally copy and paste to make it very simple for them to reach out if someone comes to mind.

Adding value is easy. Pick one person in your network, maybe someone you have not spoken with in sometime. How could you add value to them today? Maybe send them an interesting article, video, book, or even just a personal note inquiring how their latest project is going. Be the guy or gal who adds value just because it is who you are, not because you are doing it to get something in return. Now, on to the steps you have to "get right" to create your ideal clients, and engage with them courageously and boldly to not just get what you want, but give what they need.

For me as a coach, the engagement process is vital to creating and establishing solid relationships and expectations with my clients before we even begin our work together. Sometimes I connect and engage with potential clients only to weed them out as I learn and find that they really are not who I would like to work with. Other times I connect and engage with them multiple times because of where they are in life. Engagement should be your number one marketing activity and you should be spending eighty percent of your time on it each week. It is also the hardest piece of what you will do. It is a process, but if you can learn to master it and to harness the power in building relationships, you and your business will soar with every courageous and bold connection, and with the engagement you have with possible clients.

"Think twice before you speak, because your words and influence will plant the seed of either success or failure in the mind of another." -Napoleon Hill

Own It

Own it. Those are the words I had to tell myself early on in my entrepreneurial adventure. I for sure was *not* an expert, I for sure didn't feel very influential, and I was shaking in my boots most of the time. Even sometimes now, I will take on a client or a project that scares me to death. I have learned, when I feel like that, it means I am on the right path. It also means I have to repeat, "*Own it, own it, own it,*" over and over and over again. Becoming influential doesn't mean you fake it until you make it or that you wait until someone tells you that you are now influential. Becoming influential in your niche means staying the course for the long haul. It means proving yourself many times over. It means staying in a place where you are constantly learning, willfully sharing that knowledge with others, and it means you do "it" anyway, afraid or not. When you can become known as a giver, not a taker or a matcher, but as a servant driven, highly competent and integrity filled person in your area of expertise, then you get passed the crown and scepter of "influencer." However, none of this can happen if you are waiting for someone to give you permission to go for it, permission to succeed, or permission to own it. Nowhere along the journey of creating success as an entrepreneur is a "permission giving officer" waiting to bestow upon you this gift. You have to simply claim and take permission to be powerful and to thrive in your endeavor.

The piece that trips up most entrepreneurs as they build their influential reach is the, "staying for the long haul." I am sure this can be attributed to many things but the two I see most often are, lack of planning—expectations are out of control and not on a realistic time frame, and not entering into entrepreneurship understanding the gigantic mental hurdles they will be faced with daily. My advice is for you to plan everything out, all the details, and give yourself double the time you think it will take to implement and to reap the rewards, and make a commitment to stay the course. One way you can do this is to invest in your personal development. Make a plan of how you will do this each month, each quarter and each year. Which books will you read? Which workshops, retreats, or seminars will you attend? Do you need a mentor or coach?

Another area entrepreneurs seem to face is the lack of knowledge or understanding that yes, they in fact *are* sales people and there is always, always, always a sales element in each business. Many times, I hear people say they don't like sales, they aren't good at sales, or they don't want to do sales. The long and short of it is that you *have* to do sales, you *need* to learn to love sales, and you need to get *great* not *good* at sales.

Here are ten things to remember about sales:

1. Sales is just part of the game.

2. Everyone who is successful sells something, and if you want to be a successful entrepreneur and not living in your mother's basement, then you will have to do it too.

3. You can find your sweet spot and create sustainable sales systems for yourself.

4. Sales begins with your mindset, so make sure it is free from clutter, junk, and beliefs that don't serve you around sales.

5. Sales is not simply about "attracting clients," . . . it is about creating them.

6. Don't confuse time versus value because they are not equal.

7. Prices are simply filters for gaining the clients you do want and to keep out the clients you don't want.

8. Your potential clients buy what you have because of the possibility "*it*" or *you* will create for them, not because of the price point.

9. Selling is learning timing and the art of the proposal. Learn the right language to speak—that which is authentic to who you are—and you will rock it.

10. Not everyone you give a proposal to will say yes, but not everyone will say no either.

Do not become attached to the outcome, no matter if they say yes or no. If you become attached to the outcome, you will place yourself on an emotional sales roller coaster and it isn't the fun kind.

Becoming an "influencer" is a choice. It is you deciding to stay the course and do the things that make you scared, in spite of the fear. It is you pushing through the rough patches, doing the personal development, and keeping up on what is working and what isn't in your niche, and it is you owning your dream and telling anyone who questions it to either get in the arena with you or keep their opinion to themselves. It is you owning that you have a voice and a message that only you can deliver to the world. Becoming an "influencer" isn't for the faint of heart, it is for those who are willing to dig deep, find their inner super hero powers, fearlessly and courageously engage with the world, and own their message. I believe in you.

About Andrea Sullenger

Andrea Sullenger is mix of "kick butt" sales/marketing coach and inspirational possible-i-tarian. She has been working with solo-entrepreneurs for the past seventeen years, helping them build their own thriving businesses while creating a life they love. Andrea is a nationally known speaker and coach, and an internationally published author. She is a creative, out-of-the-box thinker who will challenge you to go after a BIG life and a BIG business.

Learn More Here:
AndreaSullenger.com

Continue the Conversation on . . .

Facebook: Facebook.com/andreasullengercom

Chapter 3

Mastering the Art of Delegation
by Tonya Thomas

J was speaking with a client recently, and we were discussing delegation. He made the remark that someone didn't know how to truly be a CEO because he didn't delegate the things he should. I value his opinion as he has many years in the corporate world and runs his own successful business. He's right; you do need to know how to delegate if you wish to be a great CEO. It's important to know how to release things that don't really require your attention.

Think back to when you first started your business. It was probably a very exciting time for you. However, sometime after getting started, you realize it's going to take a lot of hard work to fill your business with clients and make it successful. Even so, you're determined to make this work, so you work hard marketing your business and putting in long hours to get it off the ground. At some point things begin to pick up and before long, you realize you've achieved your goal of filling your business with clients. You feel a great sense of accomplishment. You're servicing your clients and feeling successful, but you're also working longer days and not getting everything done. You've filled your business with clients and now that has become your main focus, which is great, but your business isn't getting the attention you were once able to give it prior to filling your business with new clients.

The newsletter you were sending out on a weekly basis hasn't been sent out in two months. The business cards you've collected from various conventions and networking events are sitting in a pile in a drawer, and you haven't followed up with any of these contacts. You're missing appointments because you failed to get them on your calendar. Your website and blog are in desperate need of updating, and the list goes on. You know that in order to have a balanced, prosperous, and growing business, you will either have to work more hours, which you can't do because you're already maxed out on time, or get some help. However, the thought of someone, other than yourself handling anything to do with your business is a scary thought. What if they mess things up? You can't afford to have your business look bad, so you press on and push the thought of additional help to the side for later. Until you realize your business has come to a standstill. You business revenues aren't growing. In order to take your business to the next level you will have to bring someone else on to help you. Does any of this sound familiar? No matter how hard you work, there are only so many hours in a day. At some point, you will definitely need to begin releasing some of your workload in order to grow your business and maintain your sanity. Letting go and delegating can seem scary, but it doesn't have to be. You can learn to delegate and continue to have a prosperous business.

Prior to moving forward in your quest to delegate, you need to determine the reason(s) why you want to delegate the task(s) in your business. Is it to delegate the non-revenue generating tasks required to run your business, so you will be free to take on more clients? Do you wish to delegate in order to spend more time with your family? Please create a list of the reasons you want to delegate and what you wish to achieve through delegation. This step is important because you will want to reference this list six months to one year after you've begun delegating, to ensure you're meeting your goals. This will be a great measuring tool to the success of your delegation process.

I will be honest; delegating does require some work on your part. You may be thinking that's one more item to add to your already full to-do list. However, the rewards far outweigh the time and effort that are involved in delegating. There may be several reasons as to why you may feel you can't let go and delegate. I will cover three of the main reasons people don't delegate. One of those reasons is fear of allowing someone to "invade" your privacy. You may feel uncomfortable having someone know the inner workings of your business. As business owners, we all have things that are proprietary to our business. How we market, client information, etc. are all very private things that relate to the operation of our business. If you feel strongly about the protection of your privacy, you could address this with your attorney. Let him or her know you're considering hiring someone to help you in your business and you want to know how to protect your privacy should you add someone to your team.

Another issue business owners have with delegating is trusting that the person they delegate to will follow through with the tasks assigned. You've probably heard the old saying, *"If you want something done right, do it yourself."* However, you can't take on that mantra or you will never become a great delegator and grow your business. The key is to take your time in your search of an assistant and ask the right questions.

Current Workload

Definitely inquire if she has the availability to handle the tasks you wish to delegate. Ask how much time she has each week to handle your tasks.

Turnaround Time

If you're going to work with a virtual assistant, ask what the average turnaround time is for tasks. You can also tell the virtual assistant what you expect when it comes to turnaround time. If you would like to things to be completed within a twenty-four hour time frame, explain this to the virtual assistant, then allow them to comment on whether or not they can accommodate that time frame.

Office Hours

Another question to address is office hours. Not everyone keeps the same work hours. Be sure and ask if the virtual assistant has set work hours. Keep in mind the time zone as well. For example, if you're on East Coast time and the virtual assistant is on Pacific time, he or she may begin their workday three hours after you do. Also, be sure and ask if the virtual assistant responds to e-mails or calls outside of their hours.

Vacation Time

You should also address how the virtual assistant handles when she will be out of the office. Will she let you know in advance when she will be away, and if so, how much notice will she provide?

Communication

How will the virtual assistant communicate with you? Will it be primarily by phone or e-mail? This may seem unimportant, but if you're a heavy phone person and the virtual assistant prefers e-mail, it could become a problem. Also, do they have a system set up to check in with you regularly just to see how things are going? If not, you should definitely do this on your end. Ask the virtual assistant how he or she would feel about a weekly touch-base phone call. If the virtual assistant isn't open to this, you should keep this in mind when considering your decision about whether or not to work this with virtual assistant, as communication is very important in a successful virtual relationship.

Conflict Resolve

Ask the virtual assistant how they handle conflict when it arises in the working relationship. Do they just send you an e-mail or do they pick up the phone and discuss the issue with you? It's important to discuss this because as in any relationship, conflict is bound to arise at some point and you want to know each other's preferences on how it's handled.

Asking all of these questions during the initial interview will help you build a level of trust with the assistant you hire. Building trust will be vital in the process of delegation.

Another issue most business owners have with delegating is the cost. Don't let money be the cause of you not delegating. You may feel you can't afford to hire someone to delegate your tasks to; however, your business will not be able to move forward and generate more revenue without the additional assistance. Think of it as an investment in the growth of your business. Not only will the bottom line of your business grow, but you will also be able to spend more time with your family and do the things you enjoy doing outside of your business. To help with your fear of wondering whether or not you can afford to hire someone to delegate to, be sure and do some number crunching to determine how much you can afford to allocate each month for an assistant. This will provide you with a budget to begin with when you're doing your search for an assistant.

Okay, I've convinced you that delegation is the key to running and growing a successful business, so now you're ready to move forward. There is a process that should be followed in order to be successful at delegation. First, you should determine the tasks you wish to delegate. To do this, think of all of the things you're doing in your business that you either don't like doing or aren't very good at doing.

For example, if you're a business coach, scheduling client's coaching sessions, developing and sending your newsletter, updating your blog or social media profiles, etc. are all things you don't have to do yourself. Your main focus and attention should be on coaching your clients, which is where you shine. You could make a list of everything that doesn't involve you coaching, and all of these things are what you should delegate. If you want to start small, just pick one thing on the list with which to begin.

This will allow you to get your feet wet, so to speak, with delegating, and you can work your way up as your level of confidence grows. As you make your list, you may be thinking you can do these things on your own. Please try to stay out of that mindset. Yes, you may be able to do the tasks; however, remember that you doing them is not the best use of your time. It may take you three hours to put your newsletter together, but a more skilled assistant can do it in one hour. Also consider your hourly rate; it's much wiser to spend your time/hourly rate on client work versus administrative work.

Delegation allows you to make the best use of your time and skillset.

So, you have your list and you're thinking, *now what do I do*, right? Now you should begin searching for an assistant, if you don't already have one. If you do have an assistant you should make sure he or she is doing all of the things on your list. If he or she can't do everything on your list, you should begin a search for an additional team member(s) to delegate the remaining items on your list. If you do not currently have an assistant, your main priority should be to find an assistant. If you work from home and do not want to have anyone invading your private space, you could look into hiring and working with a virtual assistant. He or she will work from their own office and provide administrative support to you.

There are many virtual assistants to choose from, so my suggestion is to ask friends and colleagues for referrals.

You've found an assistant you feel is a good fit for you. The next step is to schedule a phone call with your assistant to discuss the tasks she will do for you. Each of you should have the list in front of you during the call. Go down the list and for each task(s) provide your assistant with your expectations for the end result. If you're working with a virtual assistant, there should be no training involved as he or she should already be skilled in the tasks which you will be delegating. However, you will need to ensure that the person who you're delegating to clearly understands what you need done and when you would like the task to be completed. For example, if your assistant will be managing your calendar, communicate the earliest time that you will accept an appointment and the latest time you will accept an appointment, etc. If your assistant will be handling your newsletter, you will need to let him or her know which day(s) and the time it should be distributed. The main thing is that your assistant knows how to support you. Ensuring a successful working relationship will require communication from both parties.

Once you've assigned the task(s) to your assistant, make sure you maintain an open line of communication. Your assistant will need for you to check in with her form time to time. Make sure you're always available should she have any questions. It's imperative that you establish a regular phone call. During this phone call be sure to discuss all tasks that have been delegated. Be sure and cover the dates of all deadlines, any issues that may have formed since the last phone call, and any other pertinent information. It's also good to discuss goals you may have for each task, and it's important to let your assistant know you wish to be made aware of any problems that arise for any task she is working on. She should let you know of problems as they arise and not after they have occurred. Let her know she can contact you outside of your scheduled calls should she need to do so.

Having this call with your assistant keeps you in the loop as to how things are progressing, and lets your assistant know you care about the work he or she is doing.

One thing to keep in mind when you're delegating is to be realistic in your expectations. Don't expect your assistant to be able to do the impossible. A good assistant will do her best to support you, but be realistic in regards to turnaround times and what can be done with the resources she has with which to complete the tasks.

Another thing to keep in mind when delegating is to resist the urge to micromanage. Don't get in the micromanaging mindset, but be in more of a supportive role to your assistant. You've given your assistant the task to complete. You will have to learn to find a healthy balance of space to allow your assistant to complete the tasks, but still maintain some control. If you find you can't refrain from constant check-ins, you may want to reevaluate your trust in the person to whom you've delegated. Micromanagement is a very poor form of delegation.

Another key component of successful delegation is documentation. Please have your assistant document the process for each task you will be delegating and have your assistant send these processes to you for your files. These will come in handy in the event a new team member joins the team or in the event you change assistants. Having documentation of each task is vital; this will keep you from having to repeat your preferences to the next person who joins your team.

You now have more free time on your hands to do what you want to do in your business, but don't delegate and forget. Your assistant will still need for you to check in with her from time to time.

Being overloaded and stressed is not a great way to operate your business. I do hope you decide to take the necessary steps that we covered, and delegate. When you're focused only on the tasks that require your utmost attention and you've delegated the things that don't require your personal touch, you will be on your way to delegation success. Remember, when delegating:

- Identify the tasks you wish to delegate

- Find the right person to delegate to

- Communicate effectively.

Following the steps of delegation will allow you the freedom and joy in life that you most deserve. You will be well on your way to becoming a master delegator and operating like a true CEO.

About Tonya Thomas

Tonya Thomas is the owner of The Small Office Assistant, a virtual assistant firm. Tonya founded her business in 2001. Prior to starting her business, Tonya held administrative positions in both the construction and banking industries. She holds a bachelor's degree from Southeastern Oklahoma State University, and has completed an extensive 20-week training course for professional virtual assistants through AssistU. Tonya lives with her husband and two sons in Dallas, TX.

Learn More Here:
SmallOfficeAssistant.com

Continue the Conversation on . . .

Facebook: Facebook.com/tonya.thomas.37819
Twitter: Twitter.com/ tonyathomas

Chapter 4

The 6 Simple Stages
of Business Planning
by Angela Warr

*B*usiness planning is an exciting, engaging, and rewarding process. As an emerging entrepreneur, business planning is key for establishing business success and growth. It involves the creation of the mission and goals for your business, it allows you to formulate strategies that will be used to help you achieve your business mission and goals, and it implements, directs, and monitors all the steps in their proper sequence.

In the chapter, I will share *The 6 Simple Stages of Business Planning,* which I have used to establish my business. *The 6 Simple Stages of Business Planning* will allow you to blend your life purpose and passion with business profit. *The 6 Simple Stages of Business Planning* will take you on a remarkable journey of success so you may live your full potential and thrive in your business.

As we go along, I will thoroughly explain each stage, which in turn will grant you the opportunity to personally explore your business planning process. An important part of entrepreneurship is being able to revisit and renew one's commitment to owning a business. This chapter will allow you to record your responses to various business planning exercises. Or, you may elect to purchase a notebook journal to record your responses. Thank you for reading this chapter.

I hope it will encourage you to pursue profitability in your business. *The 6 Simple Stages of Business Planning* are:

Stage 1: Define Your Life Plan

Stage 2: Develop a Business Concept

Stage 3: Set Financial Goals

Stage 4: Create a Marketing Plan

Stage 5: Write a Profitable Business Plan

Stage 6: Start Your Profitable Business

Stage 1: Define Your Life Plan

The first stage of the business planning process allows you to define your life plan and to determine how your life plan relates to your desire to become an emerging entrepreneur. Before you print your first set of business cards with a great business name and logo, you need to lay out the groundwork for business success. Do you know what it takes to become a successful entrepreneur? What are your mission and goals for your business? How do the mission and goals match your plans for your life, your family, and retirement? If you answer these questions before you begin your emerging entrepreneurship journey, your business will have a greater chance of success, profit, and survival.

Becoming an emerging entrepreneur involves much more than just starting a business. Entrepreneurship is a process that allows you to pursue an opportunity, use various resources, and initiate change to create value in the marketplace. Entrepreneurs are leaders who see problems as opportunities, take action in response to the problems, and accept to take on the risk in hope of solving the problems. They look for problems that customers will pay them to solve.

Entrepreneurs are driven to control their own lifestyles and bring their business dreams to the marketplace. They see opportunities in the midst of chaos and act while others may procrastinate.

As you begin to define your life plan, it is important to understand what it means to be an entrepreneur. In a quiet location, please answer the questions below:

- What is your meaning of entrepreneurship?

- What are the key characteristics of a successful entrepreneur?

- What are your entrepreneurship traits?

- What is your personal vision for your life?

- What is your personal vision for your family?

- What is your personal vision for your retirement?

- How does your personal vision for your life, your family, and your retirement relate to your dream of becoming an emerging entrepreneur?

- What is your business concept and does this concept fit into your life plan?

- What problem will your business concept solve in the marketplace?

Stage 2: Develop a Business Concept

Ideas for launching new businesses are unlimited, but your business concept must match both your life plan and the financial goals you have set. Please note that your business concept may change over time as you learn more about the marketplace and the economics of your new business. You must be willing to listen attentively to the marketplace and review your financials on a regular basis.

According to BusinessDictionary.com, a business concept is an idea for a business that includes basic information such as the service or product, the target demographic, and a unique selling proposition that gives a company an advantage over competitors. A business concept may involve a new product or simply a novel approach to marketing or delivering an existing product. Once a concept is developed, it is incorporated into a business plan. Now take a moment to select the positive attributes of your business concept.

Positive Attributes of Your Business Concept

	Checkmark
Does your business concept solve a serious problem?	
Does your business concept involve significant savings?	
Does your business concept fit into the existing scheme of things?	
Does your business concept attract media attention?	
Does your business concept identify a market?	
Does your business concept join a rapidly expanding market?	

Table 1: Positive Attributes of Your Business Concept

Based on the positive attributes of your business concept, what are the strengths of your business concept? Do you believe your business concept is good, but may have a flaw, and may not be marketable to consumers? Does your business concept only exist in your mindset? And, perhaps the marketplace is not large enough to make your business concept a success. Take a moment to select possible flaws with your business concept. These flaws signal the need to modify and change your business concept.

Possible Flaws

	Checkmark
No real need	
Does not work	
Potential marketing traps	
Unfortunate economics	
No protection	
Obsolescence	
Potential installation problems	
Requires education	
Requires change in consumer behavior	
Inaccurate assumptions	
Inconvenience	
Service requirements	

Table 2: Possible Flaws

How may you address or overcome the identified flaws or problems with your business concept?

Now that you've determined your business concept, please write your business concept statement below. Use the questions listed to assist you in developing your business concept statement.

- What does your product or service do?

- How is it different from other products or services?

- Who will buy your product or service?

- Why will the marketplace buy your product or service? Is the product or service different from other products or services? If yes, why is it different?

- Where will your product or service be sold?

- When will your product or service be ready to be sold?

- How will your product or service be sold?

Additional research is required to address your business concept. The product/service, uniqueness, customers, benefits, and promotions/sales may be addressed in *Stage 5: Write a Profitable Business Plan.*

Again, according to BusinessDictionary.com, a business concept is an idea for a business that includes basic information such as the service or product, the target demographic, and a unique selling proposition that gives a company an advantage over competitors. A business concept may involve a new product or simply a novel approach to marketing or delivering an existing product. Once a concept is developed, it is incorporated into a business plan.

Write your business concept statement. Combine the written statements listed above. Keep the statement fewer than 150 words. Focus on the content and use words and phrases that read clearly and smoothly.

Stage 3: Set Financial Goals

Now that you have explored your life plan, understand what it means to be an emerging entrepreneur, and have determined your business concept, let's discuss the third stage of business planning. The third stage is "Set Financial Goals." To become an emerging entrepreneur and to thrive in your business, you must set your financial goals. You will need to determine if your business concept is feasible and understand your business financing options. You will explore your startup costs, the profitability of your business concept, and your current cash flow. You will also explore what sources of funding are available for business startups.

To ensure your business concept matches your available finances, you must be as realistic and accurate as possible in startup estimates. Your startup costs estimates must take into account both your current available funds and how much money your business concept will need at startup. There are three questions, which you must answer to ensure your business concept is feasible and profitable. We will begin by exploring the questions discussed previously in *Stage 1: Define Your Life Plan.*

- Does my business concept match my life, family, and retirement vision?

- Does my business concept address a perceived need/problem in the marketplace? If yes, what is the perceived need/problem?

- Will my business be profitable?

In order to determine if our business will be profitable, we will need to discuss and determine our business financing options. We will discuss your startup costs, the profitability of your business concept, your current cash flow, and sources of funding available for business startups.

Your business must be profitable enough to cover its own expenses and still pay you a salary. Achieving your personal financial goals will require you to focus on the financial health of your business. *The Personal Financial Goals Worksheet* will help you establish personal financial goals and business profits needs that must be met.

Personal Financial Goals Worksheet

Financial Goals	Amount Needed
How much money are you willing to invest in your business?	
What portion of this investment will come from your own savings account?	
What portion of this investment will be borrowed?	
What salary do you want?	
Are you prepared to lower your standard of living until the business is established? If yes, for how long?	*Yes or No?* *Time*
Grow the business	
Buy a home	
Buy a vehicle	
Take business travel	
Take personal vacations	
Pursue a hobby/passion	
Attend school	
Save for college	
Invest in retirement	
Pay off debts	
How much could you earn investing your money instead of starting a business?	
What salary could you earn working for someone else?	
TOTAL AMOUNT*	
If the total amount listed above is greater than what you expect to earn through your business concept, you should reconsider the business concept.	

Table 3: Personal Financial Goals Worksheet

You have determined your personal financial goals; now let's focus on the business concept and its ability to fulfill your goals by using the financial statements as business planning tools. Let's explore the *Startup Costs, Profitability,* and *Cash Flow.*

The startup costs will determine how much money you will need to get your business concept off the ground. The startup costs are only incurred in the startup phase of business.

Once your business engages in sales opportunities, it has progressed through startup and into the on-going operational phase. Startup costs may be either expenditures or expenses. Startup costs expenditures are one-time costs for capital assets or vendor deposits and expenses are costs for operations that will continue throughout the existence of the business. Please record the *Startup Costs Expenditures and Expenses* for your business.

Startup Costs Expenditures

Expenditures	Startup Costs
Capital Expenditures	
• Equipment	
• Furniture and Fixtures	
• Leasehold Improvements	
• Vehicles	
• Buildings	
• Land	
Security Deposits	
• Rent Deposit	
• Telephone Deposit	
• Utility Deposit	
Other Expenditures	
Inventory (supplies you may sell to your customers)	
TOTAL	

Table 4: Startup Costs Expenditures

Startup Costs Expenses

Expenses	Startup Costs
Rent	
Computer Repairs	
Legal and Consulting Fees	
Accounting Fees	
Salaries and Wages – Training/Setup	
Benefits and Texas – Training/Setup	
Office Supplies (for example, postage)	
Business Supplies	
Printing – Business Cards, Stationery, Brochures	
Pre-Opening Advertising	
TOTAL	

Table 5: Startup Costs Expenses

To reduce your startup costs expenditures and expenses you may consider leasing instead of purchasing equipment, sub-contracting instead of hiring, starting your business at home, delay hiring dates, reduce inventory costs by having manufacturers drop costs, and reducing your salary with the expectations of increasing it later.

The profitability of your business concept will determine whether the concept is profitable or at least profitable in the future. One of the primary goals of every business is to become profitable. You may have enough cash to get your business started, but do you have enough to keep it going? Profit is what is left over after the expenses of your business have been deducted from the revenues generated by your business. The formula is:

$$Revenues - Expenses = Profit$$

Revenue is money or the promise of money you receive when you provide customers with products or services. You calculate the revenue by taking the number of products or services sold and multiplying by the price:

$$Revenue = Number\ of\ Units\ Sold\ x\ Price\ (per\ Unit)$$

Describe the revenue generating activities for your business below. Note, the price you charge often affects the number of products or services you sell. Increasing the price gives the customer the idea of increased value and you are able to sell more products or services. Did you know that retail stores often mark up merchandise one-hundred percent of cost? This markup means that every time a retail store sells something, up to fifty percent of the money collected covers the actual cost of the item. The remaining fifty percent covers operating expenses and provides a profit.

- What products will you offer?

- What services will you offer?

- What products/services combinations will you offer?

- How will your products/services be priced?

As your business continues to be profitable, you will be responsible for operating expenses. They include all of the expenses of operating the business. The *Operating Expenses* are also called overhead. These expenses are necessary to support the selling, administrative, and general expenses of your business. Many of the *Startup Costs Expenses* are also *Operating Expenses.*

Select the *Operating Expenses* that you expect to be ongoing in your business.

Operating Expenses

Expenses	Operating Costs
Cost of Goods/Inventory	
Advertising	
Bank Charges	
Dues & Subscriptions	
Insurance	
Licenses & Fees	
Marketing & Promotion	
Meals & Entertainment	
Miscellaneous	
Office Expenses (for example, Postages)	
Office Supplies	
Office Services	
Payroll Services	
Professional Fees	
Property Taxes	
Rent	
Repairs & Maintenance	
Shipping & Delivery	
Telephone	
Training & Development	
Travel	
Utilities	
Vehicle	
Other	
TOTAL	

Table 6: Operating Expenses

You will spend time researching your *Operating Expenses* and will record this information in your *Business Plan* using the *Income Statement*. Monitoring the profitability of your business means keeping track of the revenue and expenses; and tells you about the ability of your business to generate income.

Being profitable or not, your business must maintain a positive cash balance. The *Cash Flow* will give you a greater understanding of the cash flow needs of the business concept and identifies funding sources to meet those needs. *Cash Flow* tells you about the ability of your business to pay obligations and still maintain a cash reserve. You may use the *Cash Flow Report* (refer to example below) not only for reporting but also for projecting cash activity in your business.

When you test your business concept for feasibility, try to project its cash flow accurately.

The *Cash Flow Report* lists the sources of cash you expect to receive on a monthly basis. The report includes cash sales, collections from accounts receivable, equity contributions from owners, and loans from either owners or outside sources. The cash you expect to receive is added to the cash balance remaining from the prior month to total the cash available for that month.

Cash Flow Report
Example

Calendar Year (e.g., 2014)	Jan	Feb
Cash In		
Cash Sales		
Collections from Accounts Receivable		
Equity Received		
Loans Received		
Other Cash In (receipts from other assets)		
Other Cash In (interest, royalties) _____		
Total Cash In		
Total Cash Available		
Cash Out		
Inventory Expenditures		
Inventory/Raw material (cash)		
Inventory/Raw Material (paid on account)		
Production Expenses		
Operating Expenses		
Advertising		
Bank Charges		
Dues & Subscriptions		
Insurance		
Licenses & Fees		
Marketing & Promotion		
Meals & Entertainment		
Miscellaneous		
Office Expense		
Office Supplies		
Outside Services		

Payroll Expenses		
Salaries & Wages		
Payroll Taxes		
Benefits		
Professional Fees		
Property Taxes		
Rent		
Repairs & Maintenance		
Shipping & Delivery		
Telephone		
Training & Development		
Travel		
Utilities		
Vehicle		
Leased Equipment		
Other		
Other		
Paid on Account		
Non-Operating Costs		
Capital Purchases		
Estimated Income Tax Payments		
Interest Payments		
Loan Principal Payments		
Owner's Draw		
Other Cash Out		
Total Cash Out		
Monthly Cash Flow (Cash In – Cash Out)		
Beginning Cash Balance		
Ending Cash Balance		

Table 7: Cash Flow Example

Businesses need different sources of funding during each stage of development in the business life cycle—startup, operational, and growth. An accurate projection of cash flow over three to five years of business may help you predict your funding needs. Note that a business may operate for a long time at a loss, many do, but no business may operate without cash. No cash, no business.

Raising money is an art. It is an art that may be learned by emerging entrepreneurs. To become an expert at raising money you need to know about sources of money, how to find them, and how to evaluate them to determine which source is the best fit for your business. During the startup phase, you may not need money, but you may discover a time later when outside money is necessary. Whether or not you can get the money will depend on how well you have prepared for it and how you deal with the money sources.

All funding for your business will come from equity or debt financing sources. An equity funding source comes from entrepreneur contributions, private investors (i.e., angels and venture capitalists), earnings retained in the business, and initial public offerings. Debt financing sources come from loans from the entrepreneur, loans from friends and family, bank financing, lines of credit, and Small Business Administration (SBA) loans. Select the sources of funding you are expecting to use for your business and record the amount needed.

Sources of Funding

	Checkmark
Venture Capital	
Revolving Credit	
SBA Loan	
Home Equity Loan	
Friend/Family Loan	
Credit Card	
Bank Loan	
Personal Savings	
Total	

Table 8: Sources of Funding

You've established a business that matches your life, family, and retirement vision. Your business concept meets a perceived need/problem in the marketplace, and you've passed the profitability test. It is now time for you to begin *Stage 4: Create a Marketing Plan*, so that you may begin to earn revenue for your business.

Stage 4: Create a Marketing Plan

Your *Marketing Plan* is the foundation upon which your business plan is built. A good marketing plan will force you to think about your business growth potential and the amount of profit you will generate.

According to the American Marketing Association (AMA), marketing is defined as the activity, set of institutions, and processes for creating, communicating, delivering, and exchanging offerings that have value for customers, clients, partners, and society at large.

Marketing is anything you do to generate sales. It creates awareness of your products or services. Marketing presents products or services in ways that make them desirable. Your *Marketing Plan* brings together your understanding of the market, your customers, your competition, and your pricing. The Four P's of your *Marketing Plan* are *Product, Placement, Promotion,* and *Price.* The Four P's will help you to create sales consistently. Most of the information you need to develop your *Marketing Plan* is free or is priced low. You may spend time on the Internet, go to the library, subscribe to industry publications, join trade organizations, contact the local Chamber of Commerce, read government publications, and speak with potential customers.

To create your *Marketing Plan* you will need to complete the following exercises:

- *Step 1: Identify the Four P's: Product, Placement, Promotion, and Price.*

- *Step 2: Identify your target customers, the marketing tactics you will use to reach your customers, and define your marketing budget.*

- *Step 3: Set a sales strategy that fits your customers established buying patterns.*

Marketing Plan Exercises:

Step 1: Identify the Four P's—Product, Placement, Promotion, and Price.

Product

Describe the product or service you will offer. _____

_____

_____.

Explain how to product will meet the client needs. _____

_____

_____.

What geographical area will be served?_____

_____

_____.

What are the features and benefits of your product or service?

_____

_____

_____.

What is your competitive edge? _____

_____

_____.

Explain how your product will be manufactured or performed. _____

_____

_____.

Placement

Explain how the product or service will be delivered. _____

_____

_____.

Describe the distribution channels and the physical facilities (i.e., warehouse, garage, fulfillment house, office space, strategic alliance facility, or other area) needed for the movement of the product from manufacturing to the hands of the customer. _____

_____

_____.

Promotion

Develop a mix of marketing activities. Outline which advertising channels you'll use to get the word out. For example, Internet, flyers, magazines, newspapers, direct mail, telemarketing, radio, seminars/workshops, and television. _____

_____

_____.

Layout your public relations strategy. _____

_____

_____.

Review your personal and business networks. _____

_____

_____.

Price

Decide what the market will pay. _____

_____

_____.

Pricing strategy is all about pricing your product or service for your different target markets. _____

_____

_____.

Determine the list price, discounts, wholesale allowances, markdowns, payment periods, and credit terms. _____

_____

_____.

Based on positioning, decide if your product will have premium or discount pricing. _____

_____

_____.

Step 2: Identify your target customers, the marketing tactics you will use to reach your customers, and define your marketing budget.

- Define Your Customer

    Income: _____

    Location: _____

    Age: _____

Size: _____

Education: _____

Profession: _____

- Create Customer Value

Identify which qualities your customers value most and least about your product and service. _____

_____

_____.

- Marketing Tactics

Identify viral marketing using social media. _____

_____

_____.

Identify online marketing; invest in a website. _____

_____

_____.

Identify email marketing (communicate with past, current, and potential customers). _____

_____

_____.

Identify event marketing. _____

_____

_____.

Identify street marketing: fliers, handbills, and posters. _____

_____

_____.

- Marketing Budget

Now that you have decided on your marketing strategy and specific marketing tactics you are going to implement, you need to determine your marketing budget.

Step 3: Set a sales strategy that fits your customers established buying patterns.

- Sales strategy. Internet Marketing can be both creative and affordable. Select the sales strategy that is best for your business.

Internet Marketing Activities	Checkmark
Build valuable secondary Web sites that feed into your primary site.	
Carefully design your Web site.	
Develop a video for video sharing sites.	
Develop an electronic newsletter.	
Drive traffic to your website from links on other sites.	
Investigate e-commerce as a way to sell products.	
Join a networking site.	
Market your website.	
Measure your website performance.	
Put your product/business creation story online.	
Send email for promotion.	
Start blogging.	
Survey your website users.	
Use banner advertising.	
Use web conferencing.	
Volunteer for online interviews.	

Table 9: Internet Marketing Activities

Stage 5: Write a Profitable Business Plan

Your business plan is your road map to get you from where you are to where you want to be as an entrepreneur. It is a document that will help you focus and monitor all business steps in their proper sequence.

The main components of a business plan are:

- Cover Page

- Table of Contents

- Executive Summary

- General Company Description

- Products and Services

- Marketing Plan – Industry Profile

- Marketing Plan – Competitive Analysis

- Marketing Plan – Market Analysis and Penetration

- Marketing Plan – Pricing

- Operational Plan

- Management and Organization

- Personal Financial Statement

- Startup Expenses and Capitalization

- Financial Plan

- Appendices

- Refining the Plan

Remember, your business plan is a living and breathing document that you should review and update every six months in order to make sure your business is on the right track.

Stage 6: Start Your Profitable Business

There are several website resources available to help guide you as you start your profitable business. One of the main reasons for small business failure is that people have no clue about how hard it is to run a business. While being an entrepreneur may feel like a lonely road, there are several online communities that can help guide you through the journey. Thanks to technology, we have access to a world-wide-web. There are several tools available on the Internet to support you as an entrepreneur.

I challenge you to find a business planning accountability partner who will keep you accountable and focused on establishing a profitable business. Please "like" Warr On Wellness on Facebook and join our professional network on LinkedIn.

About Angela Warr

Angela Warr, Professional Life & Wellness Coach, is CEO of Warr On Wellness LLC, a coaching, consulting, events and products company that inspires others to think, live, and be well. A resident of Dallas, Texas, she has earned degrees in Mathematics, Computer Science, and Software & Systems Engineering, and is a World Coaching Institute certified life and wellness coach, educator, and motivational speaker. She is currently enrolled at Dallas Baptist University to earn her Masters in Mental Health Counseling. Email Angela at warronwellness@gmail.com

Learn More Here:
WarrOnWellness.com

Continue the Conversation on . . .

Facebook: Facebook.com/warronwellness
Twitter: Twitter.com/WarrOnWellness
*LinkedIn:*LinkedIn.com/profile/
view?id=309107998&trk=nav_responsive_tab_profile_pic

Chapter 5

The Balancing Act:
Finding the Entrepreneur In Me
By Claudia Rodriguez

*A*s my father said his goodbyes to me before I boarded the plane en route to California, he spoke to me in Spanish, our native language, *"If you would like to order something to drink just ask the airline stewardess for oranche jus plis."* I was about to embark on one of the biggest journeys of my life, my educational journey. At the time, I lived in a war torn country where nobody was safe; even school busses were being overturned and burned with children still inside. Therefore, two weeks after my seventh birthday, my older sister and I were sent to visit an aunt in California during Christmas break in the hopes that the political climate would die down during that time. It was only supposed to be a four-week visit. Nonetheless, four weeks turned into six months, which turned into a year, then ten years, and eventually a lifetime.

Learning and helping others grow is my passion, so it comes as no coincidence that I chose education as my career field. However, it was a specific teacher back in the first grade—Mrs. Hanks—who, with her love of helping, guiding, and teaching, captured my heart and mind, and instilled a desire in me to someday do the same for others. At first, as a classroom teacher, I helped children grow and learn. I taught children like myself who were learning English as a second language, but simultaneously were expected to master all the other subjects taught in school. At times, the students were afraid to go to school, because without knowledge of the English language they became a target of others' insults and jokes. I understood their fear, as I had lived through taunting, ridiculing, and criticizing by other students back when I was seven.

This pulled at my heartstrings and made me realize that I truly have a passion to help teachers as well. I wanted to help them grow in their craft of teaching, whether it be in classroom management, instructional strategies, or second language acquisition so that in turn they could teach and provide a safe environment to all of the students in their class. During this stage, I was fortunate to work in roles where I could mentor teachers and work with students in reading and writing. Later, I worked with teachers who were new to the profession in a mentoring role where I guided them on every aspect of teaching, from classroom management, lesson planning, and data analysis, to working with parents.

Through those roles and working with students and teachers, I comprehended that parents need someone they can turn to for help as well. Unfortunately, not all parents are acquainted with nor accustomed to the United States educational system, and some even feel intimidated to go to their children's school and ask questions or even speak to the teachers. What I quickly understood is that you can grant additional assistance to students by providing services that will help parents become informed, thereby empowering them to help their own children attain an education. Take a moment and visualize a three-legged stool. For students to be successful in school they have to put forth the effort, there has to be parental support at home, and of course, there has to be a good teacher present in the classroom. As we all know, a stool needs all legs to be present and engaged in order for it to work correctly. When parents, teachers, and students have a true partnership, the end result is academic success for the learner.

With a heart for teaching kids, mentoring teachers, and empowering parents, I was compelled to work as an educational consultant, providing training to parents and teachers. It proved to be rewarding, since I met many parents who were hungry for information that could help their kids. Teachers were eager to share their predicament as they are in the frontlines in the classrooms and the workload seems never-ending. It was through these conversations and working with children, that I was further motivated to work harder to provide products and services that would prove beneficial to teachers and ultimately students. So here I am, classroom teacher, trainer, lifetime learner, educational consultant, and now entrepreneur.

I never thought I would own my own business, as you know, it started with the dream of helping teachers find a way to complete all the demands the profession requires, but completion truly is not enough. My vision is to help teachers far exceed the demands and really pour into the profession, armed with passion, precise classroom management, specific engaging learning strategies, and the desire to truly make a difference in the lives of our future; the children. So with that vision in mind, Cognitive Concepts, LLC, came into existence.

People ask me all the time if I like owning my own business and I just smile. Especially because I know the next statement will be something like, "You're so lucky," or "It must be great to be at home." The reality is that being an entrepreneur is different than working fulltime. It is exhilarating and faster than ever, bearing in mind I am working on building a business for my family and myself; not just any business, but one that that I truly believe in and about which I care. Furthermore, the investment is not just monetary; it requires time, passion, patience, confidence, and creativity. Truth be told, when you work from home, the work never stops as your brain is obsessed with success.

As an entrepreneur, I've acquired many lessons about starting a business and managing all aspects of it. The life of an entrepreneur is cyclical. It has peaks and valleys both professionally and emotionally, but this venture is my dream and passion. So, the ups and downs take on a very personal nature. Moreover, through this journey I've discovered being an entrepreneur can be *stressful, confusing,* and *frustrating.* Let's take a look at why.

Stressful

Let's be honest, stress lives in all work environments! Its demands create an environment of constant pressure to perform flawlessly with constricting deadlines. For the entrepreneur, however, the demands are intensified by the unique responsibilities associated with owning a business. Entrepreneurs are driven, which leads to long work hours and frequent anxiety related to potential threats to the company and to your products and services. Generally speaking, people are their own worst critic, and of course, I am not the exception to this rule. If I am late on a deadline placed on the calendar by me, I feel the pressure mounting swiftly. I have quickly realized that being an entrepreneur means being deadline dependent. If I don't create according to schedule then I cannot move forward. Period. Typically, I'm a laid-back person; however, this type of pressure lights a fire within me because I want to see my vision, my passion, and my business grow and prosper.

Confusing

Yes, I said confusing. As an entrepreneur, you wear many hats in order to get your business off the ground, thereby making the workload intense. Depending on the situation, I am the CEO, CFO, HR department, sales person, marketing strategist, technology guru, office manager, and janitor. At times, you are "done" for the day with one specific role, yet there is plenty of work still left to accomplish, whether it is writing proposals, researching new markets, developing products, building relationships, or attending trainings. All the aforementioned business activities can leave you feeling exhausted and confused, with little time for rejuvenation, recuperation, and relaxation. Setting time aside to devote to family, leisure activities, and workouts is important and keeps your mind sharp and less confused as to which hat you need to wear to move your business forward.

Frustrating

It's happened before—I have spent weeks preparing for a conference and it is suddenly canceled due to weather. Perhaps you have planned a day of product development, only to have unexpected company and phone calls. Or my favorite, people think the term "work from home" means you're at home eating chocolate while you watch a movie in the comfort of your living room. As entrepreneurs, we work from our home office, go to scheduled meetings or appearances, as well as run errands. While it may appear that we are just out and about, we are truly wearing the different hats of our business. All those hats—although crucial to the business—devour our product creation time, thereby causing greater frustration because deadlines are not met or longer work hours are required to elevate our business to the next level.

Considering all the negatives I just mentioned, why would I want to be an entrepreneur? The beauty is that although there are some definite drawbacks to owning a business, the benefits outweigh the negatives; and the benefits are impressive!

It's Rewarding

There is no better feeling than knowing the service or product you provide is being used by the intended audience and that it is useful and effective. The feeling that you are valued for the work you do and the service you provide is like no other feeling. It makes all the hard work that I put into this business worth my time and sacrifice. Making a sale or winning a new client is exciting, especially when you know it's from your own hard work and for the benefit of your company—your passion. Turning a profit and knowing your business is progressing financially to a point of stability is extremely rewarding as well. Ultimately, success is reached when the entrepreneur is reaping both financial and emotional rewards.

It's Flexible

Once you have had flexibility in your life, it is hard to go back to a conventional schedule. It is possible that in the end, I work more hours in a day; however, it is work done on *my* time with hours that work for my family and me. If need be, I can stop work at 3:00 p.m. to pick up the kids from school without asking my boss for permission. That doesn't mean I don't work during the day or I don't make up the time not worked, because remember I still have deadlines to meet.

However, the flexibility allows me to make up the time when it is most convenient for me. Additionally, as the owner of my calendar, I now try to make it to most of my children's activities. It's just a matter of careful planning.

It's Freeing

The list of perks of being an entrepreneur is long, and freedom is in the top three for me. The freedom to do what I think is right for my business without being afraid to act due to the fear of being reprimanded. This is my business and I choose to make decisions based on my original reason for being in business: teaching children and growing teachers. In addition, with this freedom comes the freedom to work or not work, meaning I can schedule appointments, product development blocks, and trainings when they best suit me. I truly have the freedom to organize my work and schedule in a way that fits my personality best. However, it is important to note that with all this freedom I need to recognize that I am entirely responsible for my own success in this venture.

Now, before you can actually sit down to create, there are many obstacles you have to surpass. Some are daily obstacles, others are emotional, and a few are organizational. How do you get to the point where you get to create? How do you balance all the distractions and still accomplish your goals? I have discovered that before you can create, you have to find the entrepreneur in you. In the next pages, you will find the distractions I have battled with and my strategies to overcome them; maybe they will work for you!

The daily tasks on my to-do list were my greatest obstacle and it caused many headache-filled days. As my business was starting and growing, I felt overloaded with work. The business started to take on a life of its own and I was not quite ready for the demands it placed on my personal and professional day. Projects began to pile up, the number of clients grew, and tax time came before I knew it was time. As the pressure of the daily demands mounted, the walls in my office caved in on me, leaving me as if there was no way I could ever deliver on my promises. At times, I couldn't think straight with so many tasks to complete. I worried some tasks would suffer and fall through the cracks. Therefore, I would cram my schedule and overload my to-do lists, stopping only to sleep a few hours. I was running around stressing about my business, and my productivity levels declined as a result. As the pressure mounted, I termed this obstacle, *Daily Tasks Suffocation*, because there were many days I couldn't breathe until I was able to control the daily tasks. So how did I take control of the *Daily Tasks Suffocation*? I realized I had to quit focusing on too many tasks at once. On a daily basis, I was trying to juggle too many items all at once. I created a plan that worked for me. The plan consisted of the following:

Simplify

One of the most important lessons I've learned is to take care of projects and deadlines as they come to my desk. Why wait? Even if the deadline is far off, take care of your business in a timely manner. However, sometimes there are multiple items to take care of at once. So, what do you do then? Prioritize the work. Take time to discover which tasks produce the majority of results. Find a way to complete these tasks with little effort. Will a schedule, proposal, or a worksheet you created for one project help you with a different one? More than likely you will not have to reinvent the wheel every time; just alter it to fit the current needs.

Next, simplify by creating efficient systems that will enable you to work faster working methods. This is extremely helpful with repetitive projects such as:

- Bookkeeping and taxes

- Invoicing and accounting

- New customer inductions

- Web maintenance

Outsource

The need to control everything regarding my business has been a problem. I thought I was the only person who could work efficiently. Unfortunately, controlling *everything* leads to several problems, such as taking longer than expected to finish a project because what you are working on is not your expertise or because you are a perfectionist. It's easy to fall into the trap of wanting to perfect before making it available to the public. This is actually a huge waste of your time. Focus on creating a great product and releasing it. Even if that means you outsource parts of the product. One finished product is worth far more than hundreds of unfinished products, and since I wanted to grow my business I had to learn to let go and delegate. As I started letting go, I was able to attract and close more business, which of course led to more income.

My advice is to figure out what your strengths are and work within your core competencies. Are you the technical force, the writing guru, or the business developer? After I determined my passion and strengths, I was able to define which tasks I wanted to complete. Meanwhile, it became apparent which tasks were the ones for which I needed to hire outside support. In talking to other business owners, some suggested the use of virtual assistants, interns, and consulting companies. For me, it was about trust. Who was it I could trust and share the excitement of my business with, and who wasn't afraid to work? That is how I tackled finding the right people to hire and with whom to outsource some of the work.

Prioritize

Structure in your schedule is the key to your success. As an entrepreneur, you have to learn to work proactively, instead of reactively. Putting out fires instead of planning your success equals burnout and delay. Establish a routine such as: wake up, work out, eat breakfast, answer emails, attend to phone calls, and then block out time for your actual work. During your work time, do not check emails, answer phone calls, or sneak off to Facebook. Once your work is done, and only then, set time aside again to answer emails and phone calls. Then you are done for the day.

What I have discovered is that I actually have to turn off my cell phone, as it becomes a distraction and a time waster. This is especially true when I break out of my structured routine to answer emails and phone calls. Accomplishing my work and eliminating wasted time allows me to carve out dedicated time for family, friends, and myself.

Focus

My biggest pitfall is multitasking. I used to think I was great at multitasking projects, phone calls, trainings, etc. Perhaps there are a few gifted and talented mothers, who are not only capable of multitasking, but seem to have perfected the craft. However, for the rest of us mere mortals, we need to drop the idea that we can multitask and be effective. The brain isn't equipped to do two tasks well at once. You will end up wasting more time trying to correct your words or rewrite your email. Your brain loses productivity each time it hurdles to a new task. Focus on one thing at a time, complete it fully, and then move to the next. This will help you gain much more time in the long run.

Unplug

Smartphones are amazing, but we have to learn how to unplug at certain times of the day so we can be productive. I do think it is incredible that I can work anywhere I am because I have my phone with me 24/7. However, all the connectivity can be disruptive to your workday. All the text dings, email buzzes, and phone rings can stop your workflow and you can become unproductive as you try to attend to all of those interruptions. Truly, to work smarter you need to figure out a good time to block yourself off from your smartphone. All those noises and vibrations your phone makes will take the creativity out of your brain. The bottom line is that only *you* have the power to shut yourself off from the smartphone world in order to devote your time to the growth of your business.

Rest

Remember to take care of yourself by resting and taking breaks. I used to think there was no way I could rest because there was so much to do. Rest, in my mind, was a luxury I could not afford. Yet, I would run around stressed all day long with no time to eat, think, or have a conversation with a potential customer. I barely took time to breathe, much less sleep. My husband asked if I was going to slow down at some point because he knows that I need rest to function at one-hundred percent. Suddenly, it was obvious what I was doing wrong. I was reacting to my business not planning my daily schedule ahead of time. The reality is, this has everything to do with structuring your day so that you can take breaks. Your daily schedule needs to have blocks of time to allow yourself to rest and reset, as that will lead to success by avoiding the constant go, go, go followed by burn out. Ensure that you have time for quick walks, lunch, and brain breaks which allows you to recharge your body and brain. In addition, find what you need specifically to feel rested in the long run. In my case, I need time to read and escape into my book. Reading calms my nerves and feeds my soul. Lately, I have also discovered that about exercise as well. It provides a physical release to my stress, but also makes me feel like I can accomplish anything. It helps build a positive mind and body. Therefore, I schedule time throughout the week to read something I enjoy for fun, but I also schedule time to workout, as my mind and body need the positive outlet. Rest can look different for you; find out what *you* need in order to feel rested and rejuvenated throughout the day and week, and add it to your calendar.

Being able to simplify, outsource, prioritize, focus, unplug, and rest has been a lifesaver for my business. Implementing all six of these tactics into my work has allowed me to avoid stress, be more productive, have a clear vision, and still have time for my family and friends. With this plan in place, the focus has shifted from, *"Am I really going to be a business owner?"* to *"I am working hard and through it all I am finding the entrepreneur inside of me."* No longer do I doubt if I can do this; now I am stronger, confident, and ready to take the next step to move forward with Cognitive Concepts. With the next steps toward growing my business come some strategies that are being implemented and are at the core of my business philosophy. These approaches are what have made me find the entrepreneur inside of me.

Know Your Customers

I have learned that as an entrepreneur, you really need to know your customers. You need to know down to a science what they want, how they behave, and their aspirations. Indeed, you need to have analyzed the size of the market or how many other customers fit the target profile so you can focus on them as well. However, that is not what I am talking about. As an entrepreneur, I have come to understand that it is not enough to know your customer in an analytical manner. You must also know their names, ages, gender, education, associations, number of children, likes, and dislikes. Listen to them as they talk, but really listen. When you talk with them, remember what they have said, and genuinely ask about their kids or their favorite sport teams. Part of building a business includes the human aspect of it all. Your customers are human, just like you, and they too enjoy talking about their families and their hobbies. Of course, that will not be the main topic of conversation, as you have business matters to discuss. However, most people like to do business with those they know, like, and trust. It sets you apart from everyone else in your industry or field. Unfortunately, this does not come naturally to everybody. If this comes naturally to you, as it does to me, you're in good shape. If it doesn't come naturally to you to be personal, then you will need to practice. The key is asking about their likes because you care. Building rapport should be about two people talking and finding common ground, but in order to find common ground you have to *want* to get to know somebody. It can come across as fake or rehearsed if this is not a natural trait you possess. Remember though, emotional intelligence is just as important as intellectual intelligence when building your business.

Plan and Execute

I am the epitome of a planner. That is a good trait at times, as well as an area of struggle for me. I like to plan, because I want it to be perfect. My time is well spent on planning a project or even my day.

Unfortunately, planning becomes a problem when all you do is spend time planning. Planning is like solving a puzzle. You look at all the pieces and determine where each piece fits perfectly. Then you place it where it belongs. However, this can be extremely time-consuming, especially if you are a perfectionist.

For an entrepreneur, planning is important, and you should plan. Realize, however, that planning should not be an event, only a task. Recognize that you have to be at peace with the planning piece being a document that is subject to change, if necessary. Once the planning is complete, you can move on to creating and executing the plan, which *is* the event. The reality is that it is not enough to plan. A plan is only good when you put it into action. Therefore, ensure what is written in your action plan is going to be completed. Give yourself deadlines and meet them so your plan can be executed and your business can continue to grow—based on what you have intentionally and strategically designed.

Stay Positive

I have heard many times that our mind is our own worst enemy. That's probably because it makes us think some very odd and negative thoughts at times. Negative thoughts are our downfall, especially because they are downright crippling. Unfortunately, once we think it we tend to believe it.

I had to overcome and overpower my own brain, the same brain that was trying to work hard at creating a business.

Daily I had to wrestle with my thoughts and remind myself of recent truths I discovered about my business and myself. Recently, I have accepted that I am a business owner, that I am a smart woman, and that my business brings value to others. I am helping teachers grow and in turn, that helps students succeed. I am bringing value to others' lives by being in business. I can truly see that people like the services and products that Cognitive Concepts provides. Unfortunately, this is a daily struggle and the cure is positivism. Remain calm and positive as you build your business; do not let the voices in your head win. If they win, your business fails.

Network

Making the right connections is the lifeline of any business. Successful entrepreneurs are well aware of this fact and make the effort necessary to network for potential vendors, business alliances, sales, and marketing, as well as making other entrepreneur friends. Regardless of the reason for networking, making real connections is vital for business development and growth. This is a difficult for task for many, as meeting people proves to be a chore. For some it is second nature. I am personable; however, I am also an introvert by nature, and find networking to be painful at times. Truthfully, being selective helps. I try to only attend events that are exclusive to teaching teachers and students, as they are my passion, and talking about my passion is easy. I target certain events, and others I shy away from because it also takes me away from creating products for my customers, providing training, or mentoring teachers. As I enter the networking event and decide who I will go and talk to, I think to myself how can I be of service to that person. When I remind myself that my goal is to help others with my business, it becomes much easier to talk to potential customers or business alliances.

As I grow into the entrepreneur, I am supposed to be, and as I get to know my customers, plan and execute, stay positive, and network, I am reminded of why I started this business. I have a heart for teaching kids, mentoring teachers, and empowering parents, all for the sole purpose of helping second language learners like myself become successful in their educational career and beyond. This is what I keep in the forefront of my mind as I move from daily tactics to business development strategies that will move my business forward. The children are the fuel to my passion. I am still learning and growing when it comes to being an entrepreneur, as you can never stop learning. However, each day, planning and strategizing is a step in the right direction. Just keep moving forward with the reason why you started your business in the forefront of your mind.

About Claudia Rodriguez

As an educational professional, I am passionate about ensuring student success and helping teachers be the best they can be. My experience includes classroom teaching, coaching, and consulting. A native Spanish speaker, I have extensive experience in elementary dual language programs and English as a second language.

I am the founder of Cognitive Concepts, LLC, a company devoted to helping teachers and, ultimately, to helping students.

Learn More Here:
CognitiveConcepts.org

Chapter 6

The Characteristics of the
Entrepreneur Equation
by Dondra Bassett

*T*here is a strong battle of focus between what you need to do, and the feeling that you will never reach the dangling carrot in your face . . . the end result. I want to help you navigate the expectation of where you are with where you want to be.

At any given point, when this two-part question, *"WHAT are your goals and what is your plan on HOW to get there?"* is asked to anyone—be it an entrepreneur, business professional, student, teacher, community leader, politician, or stay-at-home parent—it can act as a throbbing tooth ache or a restless baby who can keep one up at all night.

So as you're reading this, you might be asking yourself, *"What is the relevance of this two-part question and how does this question impact me as an entrepreneur?"* It is simple; too often as an entrepreneur the focus is on the "WHAT" and the "end results." I see the huge disconnect for the entrepreneur chasing the "dangling carrot in their face" is due to the fact that they are focused so much on the end results that they do not focus enough on *how* to get there. Does this sound familiar? Maybe or maybe not!

You may be one of the following:

- **Emerging Entrepreneur**—you have clearly defined the "WHAT" of your business goals and pretty much have a clear picture of "HOW" you plan to achieve your business goals. But for some reason, you find that your "HOW" continuously seems to be trapped in a vacuum that is literally sucking up your activity without you having control and/or direction over the outcome.

- **Hybrid Entrepreneur**—you have identified the "WHAT" of your business goals and you have an unblemished vision of what you want your end result to be. But, you find yourself stuck in a place of ambiguity when it comes to the "HOW" activity which leaves you feeling frustrated, and the word *never* seems to have mysteriously moved its place card beside the words *achieving goals* at the dinner table of your business goals, and these three words are now the guest of honor.

- **Novice Entrepreneur**—you're that entrepreneur who has not identified the "WHAT" of your business goals, and even thinking about the "HOW" becomes so overwhelming that the mere thoughts have you going in circles. Nevertheless, what is flawless in your mind is the end result. You know where you want to be and you have the strong, burning desire bottled up inside of you, pushing to get out. But, that desire is crippled by the unknown of clearly defining the "WHAT" and the "HOW."

Note: As you read through this chapter, I want you to think about the aforementioned characteristics of the entrepreneur, and which features really describe *you* as an entrepreneur

Do I have your attention? Do any of these characteristics fit you and/or describe that dangling carrot you are finding yourself chasing day in and day out? My gut tells me "*Yes.*" Great! Let's look at the step-by-step process to conquering that strong battle of focusing on what you need to do to achieve the goal (the "HOW") and feeling like you will never reach the dangling carrot in your face (the end result).

My advice is pretty simple, and it follows along the four basic mathematical operations of addition subtraction, multiplication, and division. It is about defining the steps of your "*Entrepreneur Equation*" in order to achieve (equal) your desired result. Now, keep in mind, I understand that with any equation, the operations to reach the result (answer) can become very complex as you add additional values.

In fact, the scenario can change from a *simple equation* of 1+1 to a *polynomial equation* of $x^3+2x^2-x = x(x^2+2x-1)$, which will leave most people scratching their head and throwing in the towel. As with any simple or complex equation, it is about:

- First getting an understanding of the "ask"

- Defining the steps to take to achieve the ask—by understanding the rules of each operation, e.g., working within the parentheses first to find that value, before moving to the next operation

- Lastly, just doing it. Really, just *do* it, e.g., think about the times you were a student in a math class and you did not get the answer correct on the test or homework quiz. Nevertheless, the teacher/instructor was willing to give you credit just for working through the steps. The rationale is that even though the answer you provided may not have been correct the first time, the idea that you were able to conceptualize the process served as a clear indicator to the teacher/instructor that with continued practice and another opportunity, you would more than likely get the answer correct on the next test.

Now that I have discussed why entrepreneurs keep chasing the "dangling carrot in their face" by focusing more on the end results versus *how* to achieve the end results; defined the characteristics of entrepreneurs in this position; and gave you an overview of the *entrepreneur equation* concept, let's do some deep diving into the four basic mathematical operations of addition, subtraction, multiplication, and division, defining what these operations can mean to you in developing your personal *entrepreneur equation*.

Step 1—Defining the Entrepreneur Equation

If you look at the table below, titled "Entrepreneur Equation," you will find that it is broken into four distinct parts: *addition, subtraction, multiplication,* and *division*. Each of these has a definition that represents "HOW" to navigate through the task (see definitions in the "Entrepreneur Equation: Operations" table, below).

Entrepreneur Equation

Operation	Definition
+	Operation of Adding Single Additional Task in Order to Achieve the Desired Result
-	Operation of Subtracting/ Deprioritizing Task in Order to Achieve the Desired Result
X	Operation of Adding Multiple Tasks in Order to Achieve the Desired Result
÷	Operation of Dividing / Reallocating Task in Order to Achieve the Desired Result

Note: The tasks within each operation can vary depending on the "WHAT." Sometimes the tasks within the operations can run concurrently, depending on the desired outcome.

Entrepreneur Equation: Operations

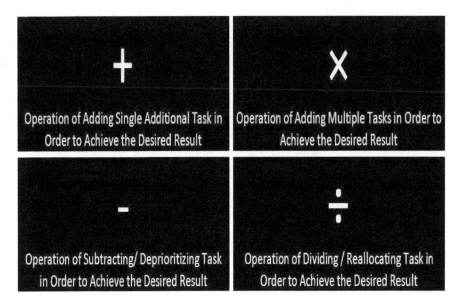

+	X
Operation of Adding Single Additional Task in Order to Achieve the Desired Result	Operation of Adding Multiple Tasks in Order to Achieve the Desired Result
-	÷
Operation of Subtracting/ Deprioritizing Task in Order to Achieve the Desired Result	Operation of Dividing / Reallocating Task in Order to Achieve the Desired Result

Step 2—Reviewing the Characteristics of the Entrepreneur

Since you have read through the four definitions of what each operation represents, let's take a step back. Remember that toward the beginning of this chapter, I asked you to consider which characteristics best describe you as entrepreneur? Let's pause for a second . . . okay, do you know which type of entrepreneur you currently are? It's ok if you don't. I will still take you through the entrepreneur equation concept and from there, maybe you will be able to identify where you might fit in.

Step 3—Each Operation of the Entrepreneur Equation

Addition: Operation of Adding a Single Additional Task in Order to Achieve the Desired Result

Entrepreneur Goal + (Additional Task) = Desired Result
WHAT + HOW (Input) =Desired Result (Output)

This operation seems relatively self-explanatory. You are an entrepreneur who has defined the "WHAT" of your business goals and you pretty much have a clear picture of "HOW" you plan to achieve your business goals; or, you're somewhere in the middle or at the other end of the spectrum, and the "HOW" activity still needs to be revisited—at least on a quarterly basis—to make certain the "HOW" activity is aligned with the overall vision and the entrepreneur goal. For instance, I will take for granted that most of you at some point have (or still do) worked for a company, and usually companies have annual meetings since they operate off of a calendar year or fiscal year. There is typically some type of "kick off" meeting and activity surrounding the goals for the year. Then throughout the given year (usually quarterly), there are reminders of the goals, and sometimes—based on strategic initiatives—the goals are realigned and adjusted from what they were, to fit the current climate changes such as, financial, stakeholder, and branding etc.

The same can hold true with your business. It may be small in size (a one-man show), growing, and thriving in its current market, or it may still be in its early conceptual stages. Still, it very important to carve out time—setting a schedule on a weekly, monthly, quarterly and even annual basis—to revisit the business goals in an effort to ensure that you're adding the appropriate task, to achieve the desired result.

Subtraction: Operation of Subtracting/Deprioritizing a Task in Order to Achieve the Desired Result

Entrepreneur Goal - (Deprioritizing Task) = Desired Result
WHAT - HOW (Input) =Desired Result (Output)

Like the addition operation, this operation is easy to understand. You are subtracting activity in order to achieve the desired results. Now in the theory, this concept seems virtually transparent. But, when thinking about it based on the actual activity, it can be like a child having to give away a toy he or she thought was his/her favorite, that is until the parents gave them an even bigger and better toy because the child was willing—willing gave up something—in order to make room for something better. That's right. Subtracting or deprioritizing tasks does not necessarily mean you have given up on the activity or the activity does not serve value.

I'd like point out that this type of activity can be common among *emerging*, *hybrid*, and/or *novice* entrepreneurs. Like the addition operation, at some point, as an entrepreneur you will have to execute this operation by evaluating the task, and making a decision. You can decide to subtract the activity for now/temporally (or maybe permanently), because it doesn't fit at the time. However, this does not mean you will not use it later in a different equation. The activity will more than likely be used again when appropriate.

Multiplication: Operation of Adding Multiple Tasks in Order to Achieve the Desired Result

Entrepreneur Goal X (Multiple Task) = Desired Result
WHAT X HOW (Input) =Desired Result (Output)

I like to think of this operation as the accelerated activity that the *emerging entrepreneur* may have a comfort level with in terms of the types of operations and tasks in this space.

Now, that is not to discount the *hybrid* or the *novice* entrepreneur by saying these folks cannot utilize this operation. All things considered, I find that all three groups tend to make this place a permanent residence, because it feels like a space where you can be efficient and get to the desired results quicker. While this may be true in theory, if you are not careful, this space can pose as the *danger zone*. That's right, I said it: *danger zone.* You are probably asking, "*Why is this a danger-zone operation?*" I'll tell you why. Because this operation feeds into the concept of being efficient with doing more than one activity at the same time; which in most cases can be done with no problem and the results achieved quicker, relatively speaking. On the other hand, what makes this operation a *danger zone* is that many people do not have the appropriate amount of allocated resources to operate efficiently in this space. As a result, the activities in this space run concurrently with limited resources. And like any project plan with resource constraints, the project can quickly go from "green" to "red." Then the project manager will have to go back and revisit the time line in order to reassess the gaps, and come up with a new project plan that will accommodate the resource constraints in order to meet the deadlines/deliverables.

Division: Operation of Dividing/Reallocating a Task in Order to Achieve the Desired Result

Entrepreneur Goal÷ (Dividing/ Reallocating Task) = Desired Result
WHAT ÷HOW (Input) =Desired Result (Output)

This operation might be known in business as restructuring, outsourcing, or modifying activity in order to achieve the desired results. Now, I'll take for granted the *novice* business owner may not have the capital to think about outsourcing tasks. By and large, these activities will be done by the novice entrepreneur by him/herself, which is okay. However, what is key to dividing out tasks—whether you are currently a "solo act" or not—is to understand that reallocating, by definition, can mean rearranging or moving. This doesn't mean you're permanently subtracting out the task. It means you're dividing the task and other resources (or different times) in order to achieve the desired goal.

Now that we have defined each equation on a macro level, if you will, I want to bring your attention to one last point toward the strong battle of focus on what you need to do versus feeling like you will never reach the "dangling carrot in your face" . . . the end result. That goes back to the "WHAT" and the "HOW." If you noticed, when I defined the *entrepreneur equation* for each mathematical operation, the equation, for example read:

WHAT + HOW (Input) =Desired Result (Output)

Correct, and the reason this point is relevant is to bring awareness to the input versus output. Let me break it down.

The "WHAT"—In taking the time out to examine any goal, whether it be personal or business, the "WHAT" can be known or unknown, depending on the circumstances. Sometime the "WHAT" can or cannot be controlled, and sometimes the "WHAT" can change on a dime. So at the end of the day, knowing the "WHAT" is key, but where the work comes in navigating through the space of "HOW" (input).

The "HOW" (Input)—The reason why *input* is put in parentheses with the "HOW," is because this is where the action takes place. The input activity is the core or nucleus of the entire goal. As previously mentioned, this is the place many get stuck and decide to throw in the towel, because the work in this space may not have an immediate result. This can lead to unwarranted frustration and make some choose to give up. While the input space can have a "slippery slope, the upside can be so rewarding that once you understand the process of steering comfortably here, you're more equipped to move from the passenger seat to the driver seat, ready to direct the output of the "WHAT" that may come your way.

The DESIRED RESULT (Output)—This space speaks for itself. It is where all entrepreneurs want to be. This is the space of victory. It is held in high regards and can come with accolades and recognition to catapult your business to the next level. However, the *danger zone* of this space is that most entrepreneurs innately focus their time and energy here. A good example would be a business that has a website up and running. The website traffic is becoming more frequent and customers are becoming more and more interested in the product the business has to offer. The business has made complete investments into the website with the look and feel, which is great. But what the business did not do effectively was make certain the products advertised could meet the supply and demand of the customer base. So the fallout in this scenario is that while the business had a fantastic website up and running, when it came down to fulfilling the customer's order, the customer was not very successful because the business failed to focus on the "HOW" (input) of the backend systems. As a result, the business owner had less control of their outcome, which is now solely driven by the customer rather than the business, and this can have a domino effect on the business brand, financials, sales, and marketing. I use this example to say, *"Don't stop thinking about the DESIRED RESULT (output) of your goals, but shift your focus to thinking more about the "HOW" (input) to achieve these goals."*

Quick Recap:

- Remember to think about "WHAT" your goal is and what your plan is on "HOW" to get there.

- It is an easy, step-by-step process toward conquering the strong battle of focusing on what you need to do to achieve the "HOW" versus feeling like you will never reach the "dangling carrot in your face" . . . the end result.

- Ask yourself what type of entrepreneur e are you:

  o Emerging Entrepreneur
  o Hybrid Entrepreneur
  o Novice Entrepreneur

- WHAT + HOW (Input) = Desired Result (Output) Equation

- Entrepreneur Equation

Finally, I want to leave you with one of the quotes that anchor my life.

"Trying is the lowest form of commitment. Either you do it or you don't." –Unknown

When you do make a commitment to do a task, and for whatever reason you do not achieve the desired results, then revisit it and figure out how to make it work. Then do it again. Or you can make a decision to *not* commit to do the task and be okay with that. Either way, I challenge you to recondition your mind to move out of the place of saying, "*I am trying to do.*" Instead say, "*I will or will not do.*" This was you have clearly defined your commitment level toward the given task.

About Dondra Bassett

Dondra Bassett is committed to helping individuals create a personal career brand and developing a comprehensive strategy on how to do it. As the founder and owner of Bassett Career Branding Solutions (BCB), she is committed to winning and bringing out the "winner in you."

Credentials and Education:

Over a decade of experience in training, sales and marketing
Marketing Professional –eCommerce Marketing
University Professor
BA—Langston University
MBA—Leadership, Tiffin University
MA—Organizational Management, University of Phoenix

Learn More Here:
BassettCareerBrandingSolutions.com

Continue the Conversation on . . .

Facebook:Facebook.com/pages/Bassett-Career-Branding-Solutions/626141867463278?ref=hl
Twitter: Twitter.com/bcbsolutions

Chapter 7

You Are Your Business
by Gabrielle Smith

Congratulations on stepping out into the exciting world of entrepreneurship! Whether you have taken the plunge and given your two-week notice at work, or simply made the decision to materialize that idea you have been playing around with for years, as you step out and into entrepreneurship, you must invest in yourself.

When most entrepreneurs hear the phrase, "invest in yourself," they further think, *you have to spend money to make money.* This then brings on the pursuit for the shiniest business cards, an upgraded computer system, or leasing office space in the trendiest building. Though these investments may be necessary components of your business practice, they are just that—components of your business practice. They are not your business.

The aforementioned clichés are fundamental misnomers that most emerging entrepreneurs buy into. Investments in such misnomers cause many entrepreneurs to invest a disproportionate amount of energy and resources in business image and not business substance. Please hear me well when I say that business image is important, however, if the substance of the business does not parallel or exceed the image, the lack of substance will tarnish the image.

Investing in yourself goes much deeper than the acquisition of the best marketing materials and assets. It speaks to the reality that all entrepreneurs must embrace at some point in their journey that, you are your business and your greatest business asset. Tom Hopkins puts it this way, *"You are your greatest asset. Put your time, effort, and money into training, grooming, and encouraging your greatest asset."* Hopkins' wisdom shines a light on the entrepreneurial path that if heeded, can accelerate you passed the many roadblocks that would otherwise detour you from your goals.

Since I have talked about what investing in yourself is not, let's look at what investing in yourself is.

When most people think or hear the word "investing," they automatically think stocks, real estate, the stock market, and portfolios. No matter your feelings about these cues, the general understanding is that if I do something now I will secure something greater for my future. Dictionary.com describes investing in characteristics terms such as using, giving, or devoting time, talent, etc., for a purpose or for the achievement of something; to furnish with power, authority, and/or rank.

The very nature of an entrepreneur is that of an investor. Though there may be immediate results in the work of an entrepreneur, such as additional income and flexibility, the goal is typically one that is long-term in nature, such as independence, legacy, generational wealth, and security. Because the latter is often the focus, it stands to reason that the investments we make in business should be in those assets that have the most lasting return—**you**!

So how is it that you do as Hopkins admonishes—train, groom, and encourage your greatest asset? Let's move forward and answer this question.

Training Equates to Influence

Training refers to knowledge and skills gained vocationally and practically. The reason that training is critical to the entrepreneur is that the level of training will determine the level of influence. Before I go any further, this is not a fancy way of saying the more education you have the greater your realm of influence—hogwash! Knowledge and skills are not gained only through degree programs, they can be acquired vocationally and practically. Think of all of the entrepreneurs such as Bill Gates who left the confines of university halls to materialize their innovations.

So, let me repeat, your training as an entrepreneur will determine your level of influence. Influence is the power to change without force. Though it is simple in concept, it is an extraordinary feat to foster. It is easy to manipulate and force results, but it is an act of finesse to influence; to affect people, circumstances, and processes for the betterment of all. Influence is a great force and cannot be manufactured overnight. It is far greater than your number of "likes" and Google rankings.

Entrepreneurship translates to and is often synonymous with influence, but we tend to limit our level of influence to marketing and influencing others procure our goods and services. We limit our influence to a message or a slogan and hope it strikes our market to action. Now, the point could be adequately argued that this *is* the point of influence and we are seeking to bring about change. Consider this . . . the nature of influence is to possess a power to bring about change without force, however, we tend to indirectly influence and subtly force action. All action does not translate to change, especially when it is done with a sense of powerlessness.

If you understand your power rests in that which you have been trained in vocationally and practically, you will more than likely find you have more power than you think.

I am not a huge television watcher but one of my favorite shows is *What Not to Wear*. Just from the title you can gather that this is a type of ambush makeover show, but that is only on the surface. The show actually deals with people who believe they are portraying one image—such as "*Oh, I am laid back and comfortable,*" or "*Oh, I'm just not a material girlie-girl*" (a belief in disguise)—while not realizing they are actually portraying what they truly believe, such as "*I don't feel worthy enough to make a fuss over dressing nicely,*" or "*I was considered the smart one of the family and my sister was the pretty one.*" By the end of the show, the universal epiphany usually takes on the form of something like, "*I did not wan to bring too much attention to myself and make people think* (fill in the blank)."

Many entrepreneurs seem to mimic the show's badly dressed contestants, who use outdated, ill-fitting garments to fade into the background of their world, while attempting to indirectly force others to believe something they don't truly believe themselves. Office managers dilute their stellar administrative skills, and fail to translate how their administrative abilities translate into being the proprietor of their own virtual assisting firm. Executives are often distracted by the change in corporate scenery and delay their desire to organize that new professionals mentoring program in underserved communities. Stay-at-home moms wrestle with not having enough "real" experience and push away opportunities to begin a network of empty nest moms who want to pursue a career outside of the home. As entrepreneurs, we attempt to manage the influence of those safe things in our immediate surroundings, but not much more. As a matter of fact, we often equate influence to marketing and nothing more, thinking, *"What do I have to offer?"* The goal is to put the focus on the business and keep it off of the entrepreneur.

As a first generation college graduate, I entered a world I did not believe was mine. I did not realize I was showing up as a visitor and not a citizen. I was happy and grateful for the opportunities and privileges that were afforded to me, but I did not want to make a big fuss about asking for too much more or believing I could make a big difference. I believed it would be too presumptuous of me to think I had the power to change anything more than the circumstances of my family. I did not want to make too many waves and bring too much attention to myself. I didn't want others to believe I could do something I was not even sure I could—or that I had something I did not possess. My unconscious goal was to stay under the radar.

It was not until I came to learn, know, and understand that the opportunities I was given were more than just those of an education, the privilege of traveling, etc. Rather, they were about access and power, and that power would exceed the needs of my family!

It is said, to whom much is given, much is required. I have learned that what's required of me is to not only accept the power afforded me, but to use that power to bring about change. This understanding gave me the authority to do what I have been empowered to do.

Take the time to inventory your skills. List everything including those things that seem insignificant to you. Your training and skill set will give you some guidance into your place and level of influence. Start where you are. You can always invest in more training but make the commitment to start where you are and build. Someone needs exactly what you already have and they need it now.

Grooming Equates to Positioning

Like most entrepreneurs, I spent the time and energy of my initial years in business thinking I would find success and purpose by positioning myself in relationship to the latest trends and well-known trendsetters. My thought was that if I could catch the next best wave of success and ride it to my purpose, all would be well. From flower seeds to income protection (a fancy name for insurance), from Southern style home décor to eye shadows and lip glosses; you name it, I did it. I positioned myself on various paths, just as many of my fellow entrepreneurs did, who "invested" in the promise of fast-tracked success and independence, packaged in the form of coffee, laundry detergent, vitamin supplements, and energy connections. Please know this is in no way, shape, or form a jab at multi-level marketing (MLM); I have been and still am a huge fan and a supporter of such ventures. Let's face it; MLM remains one of the greatest avenues to obtain wealth and financial freedom because the systems work—period.

I would not trade those days and ventures for the world because I met great people, honed my business skills, and more than anything learned what my purpose was *not*. Henry Ford said failure is not failure but the opportunity to begin again intelligently. Well, after many failed attempts at success and being positioned in someone else's market, I realized my success would not be materialized in positioning myself in relationship to others, but rather in relationship to my purpose. I now understand those attempts were necessary stops on the path of my purpose, because they are no longer distracters to my purpose.

So what's relative about grooming and positioning? It's like putting on someone else's ill-fitted clothing and pretending they are yours; or even worse, pretending you are them. The point of grooming is that you take the time and care to "wear" what fits you and wear it well. It is the time and care you take to present yourself in your best light. If you are not a person who has values beauty and aesthetics, building and empire on cosmetics or home interiors would be fraudulent and without lasting reward. Just because someone else is successful in these areas does not mean you will be. The sooner you can realize this fact, the sooner you can discover your authentic style, and consistently groom that style and position yourself in the center of successful entrepreneurial endeavors.

Encouragement Equates to Engagement

Engagement is the place where the groundwork of influence and positioning ignite. Engagement involves:

1. Being present at a specified time and place

2. Emotional involvement or commitment

3. The state of being in gear

If there is ever a word which challenges a person to action, it is this one.

Being present is an active process. It requires your conscious attention to each given moment. It is fueled by your consistent assessment of that which is meaningful and relative to your purpose—and this is just the beginning as specificity of timing and location is most critical. Showing up at the appropriate time but in the wrong location could prove unfruitful at best.

I remember having a lunch date with a friend of mine, Dianna. We only get to see each other a few times a year so these luncheons are a treat. We are always so excited to see each other and to catch up on all the events following our last luncheon. We were conscious of the day of the event, and when the specified time arrived, we found ourselves in the right restaurant but in cities forty-five minutes from each other.

Since Dianna and my friendship is such that we value the time we spend together, we quickly decided who would stay in their location and who would travel to the other location. We were both equally willing to travel and equally insistent the other stay at her respective location. This level of emotional involvement—also known as friendship—and commitment, is a decision reinforced by our belief in each other and the friendship we share. As soon as I arrived at her location, we burst into laughter, and greeted each other with our usual embrace.

As an emerging entrepreneur, your level of emotional involvement and commitment must be a decision you reinforce daily, because it is this level of involvement and commitment that will directly determine your level of engagement and connection.

As a state of being in gear, engagement is the indication of the win-win connection for which influential entrepreneurs are known. This is the element of engagement which affirms your alignment to your purpose and those it is designed to serve. It is this pinnacle to which you rise when what you have to offer is graciously recognized and received by its intended recipient. This is the time and place in which the cycle of change and transformation are not only instituted, but also perpetuated beyond both parties' imaginations. This is the purpose for which you were born.

When you are consistently engaged with that to which your purpose is connected, you are consistently encouraged because you know that who you are and what you do is connected to a greater purpose. When you know you are connected to a greater purpose, you evaluate your life, your experiences, and who you are with greater measure. When you begin to evaluate your very existence (past and present) with greater measure, others will see that measure and stand in agreement. Suze Orman says it this way, *"If you don't value what you do, people won't value who you are."* I would like to add that when you value who you are and what you have, people value what you do.

Since this is a playbook, here are nine plays you can rehearse as you step out and invest in yourself as an emerging entrepreneur.

Nine Strategic Plays for Your Playbook

Investments in Influence

1. Keep Inventory

A great part of keeping inventory lies in you owing your power and knowing you have a level of influence exactly where you are. I have learned you get more power by using the power you have! This is not a challenge to get a degree or a certification, but rather a charge to assess what you have to offer, and become confident in *that*.

2. *Do Something*

The operative word here is *do*! As entrepreneurs, we go into seasons of planning, wishing, and hoping and can easily get stuck there. It is only what you *do* that has the ability to influence, and thus bring about change.

3. *Be Authentic*

As an emerging entrepreneur, you must show up authentically in your market to do what you say you can do. Authenticity breeds trust, and trust is the cornerstone of influence. When you foster the first two tenets, authenticity is almost automatic. As entrepreneurs, we often rack our brains trying to create ways to get our market to come to us. How about going to your market? And bring what you have and what's needed! A closet entrepreneur is a broke and non-influential entrepreneur.

Investment in Positioning

4. *Start Where You Are*

Stephen Covey wisely admonishes in his *Seven Habits of Highly Effective People* who we begin with the end in mind and I agree. Based on my experience, I would like to extend his sage advice by saying that influential entrepreneurs who are positioned for win-win engagements begin where their end began. Here's what I mean . . . mentors, coaches, and icons carry the ability to accelerate your path because they possess a treasure map that is covered with dirt, blood, sweat, and tears of *not* having known then what they are now modeling to you. In other words, they make being influential look easy. To this end, choose mentors and coaches based on their journey, not their personality or celebrity.

The cardinal mistake every entrepreneur makes at some point on their journey is they attempt to begin where they want to end. We run out and rent office space before we book our first client or sell our first product. We spend more than we should on marketing material before we have adequately identified our target market, and the gravest of mistakes is that we chain ourselves to the unrealistic expectation of having to know, be, and do everything all at once. We dehumanize ourselves and leave no room for failure, grace, and growth.

If you want to have a talk show with similar influence and effects as *The Oprah Show*, or time-tested quality hair products of Paul Mitchell, or the cutting-edge logistics systems of Jeff Bezos and Amazon, you are well within your right and potential to visualize and achieve. Here's the caveat: as you continue to aspire to those similar ends, you must also identify with Oprah's beginning days of not being a talk show host but rather refining her interviewing skills as a young, inexperienced journalist who endured long days and grueling assignments. You must identify with Paul Mitchell who lived in his car, borrowed money from his mom, and could only afford the now iconic black and white ink to label his products. You must identify with Jeff Bezos as he processed orders on the floor of his garage because he could not afford work tables. To position yourself in your market as an influential entrepreneur, you must begin where your end began.

5. Be Purposeful and Productive

As entrepreneurs, we often fall prey to the adage that we have to work as hard for ourselves as we work for others. While this is valid in the general sense, it can also invalidate our efforts. Productivity and effectiveness are not products of busyness; busyness is often a product of uncertainty and fear—uncertainty of what you are doing and fear of its success (no, not its failure). The compulsion to constantly act is often a distraction from this uncertainty and fear. You must adopt the philosophy of working smart and with certainty. You must work within and on purpose, committing only to and doing those things which are aligned with executing your purpose. Though this can keep you busy, you and your efforts will be productive.

6. *Be Known for What You are Not*

No, this is not a typo! Be known for what you are *not*! At some point in time as an entrepreneur, you accept the reality that there are many people who do what you do or something similar to it. You will also come to realize this is a good thing. When you don't realize or accept this reality, you easily fall victim to—or become perpetrator of—destroying the competition by adopting an attitude of *"since I fear joining you, I will destroy you"* (i.e. gossip, lack of support, undermining, distancing, etc.). This is the wrong position to take. You must become a student of your industry because you are a contributor.

Now with all this in mind, you can become known for what you are not. Simply stated, embrace and celebrate the difference you contribute to the market. Remember, as an influencer you do not force, you own your power to facilitate change by being that change you desire to contribute. Here's an example . . . I recently saw a movie entitled *Baby Mama* starring the dynamic duo of Tina Fey and Amy Poehler. Actor Greg Kinnear played the role of a former lawyer turned socially conscious juice bar owner. The movie was produced in 2008 and the most iconic venture similar to his was Jamba Juice. Each time a new customer would walk in the shop or he would explain his profession, the unanimous question everyone asked with glee was, *"Oh, like Jamba Juice?"* He would cringe and insist, *"No! It is nothing like Jamba Juice!"* Needless to say, by the end of the film he had accepted this aforementioned "epiphany" and began responding by saying, *"Yes, just like Jamba Juice."* The funny thing is, when he surrendered to this truth, people were able to connect to him and were converted to customers.

Investment in Engagement

7. Know Your Market

Knowing your market is a notion that is extremely easy to glaze over. Entrepreneurs tend to vacillate from believing *everyone* is their market to believing their market is invisible. Rather than getting into a duel over this matter, here's a simple, two-question litmus test:

> 1. Have you attracted more clients than you can service, and find you have to turn them away or refer them to others in your industry?
>
> 2. Have your daily, weekly, monthly, and annual profits exceeded your wildest imagination?

Congratulations if you answered "yes" to both of these questions. You know your market so please skip forward. If you answered "*No*" to either question, you must make it your business to identify your market.

Had I known this during my initial years as an entrepreneur, my treasure map would have less blood, sweat, and tear stains. As an influential entrepreneur, you must do the necessary work of matching your purpose and your market if you want authentic engagement.

Consider the following questions:

- Who am I? (This is your story.)

- What do I possess? (These are your qualifications. Resist the temptation to *solely* think certifications and degrees.)

- Who wants what I have? (This is a reference to demographics.)

- Where can I find them? (This is a reference to characteristics and lifestyle.)

Knowing your story clues you in to who you are and what you possess. Knowing your story is an important part of engagement because it cues you to your market magnetism. Throughout this chapter, I shared bits and pieces of my life and interests. Your life has given you certain sensitivities and sensibilities, and this connects you to your market.

8. Go to Your Market

Going to your market is as literal as it is figurative. Years ago, it would have been redundant to make such a statement. Many brick and mortar companies began in a briefcase, and many innovative concepts were executed in a garage. Encyclopedias, food storage containers, household products, and cosmetics were sold to customers at their front doors. Now, I am not suggesting you hit the pavement and start knocking on doors; the point I am making is that going to your market is not as far-fetched as you would think. Over the years, as our society and business practices have advanced, this practice of "going to" the customer has changed. Most businesses spend a great part of their budget getting customers to come to them, and there is nothing wrong with this. However, the onus is not solely the customer's. *You* must go to your market.

Today, going to your customer can take on many meanings. Are your customers prevalent on social media? Are they in a particular organization or association? Are they concentrated in a certain area of the community or the country? Are they found on the Fortune 500 list, in universities, in their home taking care of their families? Find out where they are and "go" to them.

9. Keep Market Pulse

Earlier I admonished you to choose principles over trends and this is a good place to delve deeper into this challenge. Truly knowing your market allows you to learn how they prefer to engage. Technology has advanced to the degree that the means and modes of communication are boundless. The advent of social media and other virtual communication platforms such as Skype and Adobe Connect make engagement possible at any place and at any time.

Although technology has opened the doors to global and instantaneous communication, it cannot replace the time-tested principles of human interaction and marketing. Principles give you the "what" and "why" while trends give you the options to decide "how." Engagement rests on values which require you to learn what your market values and to foster win-win engagement.

You cannot choose your mode of engagement by keeping your finger on the pulse of technology and social media (for it is sure to change). You must keep your finger on the pulse of your market and how they engage to the world around them. Is your market recent college graduates who could benefit from an e-course on building a job-winning portfolio? Is your market soon-to-be retirees who could benefit from an in-house seminar on managing retirement accounts and income protection? The goal is to find the pulse of what your market needs, and use the appropriate technology to meet those needs.

Congratulations once more on stepping out and into the wonderful world of entrepreneurship. May you always be reminded that you are your business and you are your greatest asset.

About Gabrielle Smith

Helping others realize their professional potentials and developing leadership abilities has long since colored Gabrielle "Gabbe" Smith's life and career. Gabrielle's training in psychology, and her industry/organization specialization has allowed her to make significant inroads into the local community of the Dallas-Fort Worth area as well as on a national level with motivational speaking and training series through her consulting firm, Visionaires.

Known as the "trainer's trainer" and the "coach's coach," Gabrielle works in particular with organizations as well as with individuals who are experiencing blocks and seemingly insurmountable hurdles, to help them achieve their goals and facilitate change.

Contact Gabrielle at:
Gabbe@visionairesconsultinggroup.com

Learn More Here:
VisionairesConsultingGroup.com

Chapter 8

Booked for Speaking Success
by Kimberly Pitts

*O*ne of the BIGGEST fears people have is speaking in front of people. I totally get it. I used to be terrified to speak in front of people. However, not for the reasons you may think. Before I jump into how to be booked for speaking success, it is important to me to share with you why I am so passionate about this topic.

When I was none years old, my entire world shifted. It seemed as if the summer between sixth grade and seventh grade changed the course of my life. At a young age, I physically grew faster than most young girls, and not in a way that makes a young girl feel confident. I recall feeling as though I went from one stage of life to the next immediately. My body changed, I developed acne, and I started to stutter when I spoke in front of large groups of my peers. Luckily, this period of time was way before the age of social media. I didn't have to worry about being videoed, or having some crazy post shared on social media, but I did have that group of girls who loved to make fun of me. They did this especially when we had to give a presentation. I remember the snickers and the giggles when I had trouble saying a word, and when I got really nervous, all my words collided like a train wreck!

So, dealing with all these changes at a young age really made me self-conscience about who I was, and how others saw me. I hated to open my mouth to speak to anyone I really didn't know. I recall feeling like every time I stood in front of people, they were looking at all that was wrong with me, and not paying attention to what I was saying. I know that as a young lady, it is not uncommon to go through things like that, but when you are equally being made fun of for stuttering and having an over-developed body, it wreaks havoc on how you see yourself.

Did I have a support system around me during this time? Yes! My parents, sister, and all my extended family were amazing and so supportive. However, it didn't matter how supportive and amazing my family was (which they were), I still had to walk through those halls each day. I still had to work through all that I was experiencing.

For years, I held in those feelings I experienced in middle school. I likened them to those funny mirrors you find at the circus. You know the ones that make you look taller, skinner, or cartoon-like . . . the ones that distort your reality? What I perceived was through the lens of that funny mirror, and through those lenses, I shaped what my perception was of speaking.

Now fast forward, and I have decided to become an entrepreneur. You see the interesting thing is that I have been in leadership positions from my youth to my adult years, but when I started my business, my leadership style had to change. It needed to change. I was very comfortable leading from behind the scenes for most of my life. I didn't have to speak to large groups of people. I didn't have to talk on the radio. I didn't have to worry about whether or not when I opened my mouth, my words would run together and cause me to stutter. There are no worries when you lead from behind the scenes. I was comfortable and very content leading in such a cozy place. However, as my business grew, God started to call me to step behind that curtain and step up into what he had designed for me. One large part of doing that was to stop turning **down** opportunities that positioned me in front of my audience sharing, educating, and equipping.

As I truly grew to accept that truth, I knew being an entrepreneur meant I had to conquer my fears. I had to work through those childhood feelings and experiences that kept rearing their ugly head. I had to uproot those memories of kids laughing and making fun of me. I had to make a decision that in order to grow my business, I needed to seek opportunities that would get my name out there. Basically, I took that fear and decided to face it. Now don't get me wrong, this season of my life was not easy, comfortable, or fun. But it was necessary. If I didn't seek those opportunities and push myself, I would have remained stagnant.

Maybe you are like I was, and you are not comfortable with speaking in front of groups of people. The idea of speaking in any format scares you. Maybe you are totally comfortable and you are just not sure what to do to get out there more. This is what I would like to cover for you. Regardless of what side of the coin you are on, speaking is the number one revenue generating activity you can do in your business.

The truth is, speaking is literally the best way to increase your visibility, credibility, and influence. You are able to share your expertise and your influence with your ideal clients. They will come to see you as an authority on the subject in which you speak. You gain greater brand recognition with your audience, the ability to connect with those you are targeting, an opportunity for your audience to get to know you, and you are able to share your expertise in various formats.

Let's look at some ways you can add "speaking" to your business.

- Host your own live events (where the public can attend).

- Host your own programs in your home (group coaching).

- Host your own radio show.

- Participate in a telesummit as an expert in your field (consider a video telesummit).

- Develop video blogs versus written blogs (people love to connect visually).

- Host your own teleseminar series.

- Host virtual events (speaking and/or training).

- Participate as a speaker at a conference.

- Participate as a speaker at networking meetings of local associations or organizations.

- Serve as a panel expert at an event.

The above ideas are just a few ways you can infuse "speaking" into your business so as to position yourself as an expert or go-to person. Spend some time thinking about how you can "speak" to your target audience.

Is this you? *"I am not a great speaker. How can I speak in front of other people?"*

Let me let you in on a little secret . . . many people are not "great" speakers. Here is what I mean. There are people who speak in a way that mesmerizes you—people who are very charismatic. What happens is that you look at these people and you compare yourself to them. Not everyone will speak or present in that manner and that's okay. You don't have to look at what a perceived "great speaker" looks like. You have to speak and present in a way that best resembles who *you* are. There are groups that can help you to speak clearly and effectively, and these groups are great.

However, I come from a different mindset. When I go to listen to someone speak, I am not concerned about how they speak, or whether they have all the bells and whistles. I am much more concerned about what they have to share. Are they delivering high value content that can help me increase my client base, my skills, and my cash flow? Are they valuing my time by providing information that can really enhance my business? That is what I personally look for. The truth is, that is what your audience is looking for.

Here's how to shift your mindset and realize that as an entrepreneur/small business owner, you have a service and purpose people need to know about. Let's look at the three areas that will set the stage for being booked for speaking success.

Speak to Serve

Remind yourself that speaking is truly an opportunity to share an important message your audience should hear and needs to hear from you. When viewing it as an act of service rather than of self-promotion, you keep your focus on those you're speaking to and seeking to help. This mindset brings you back into alignment with your purpose as to why you are an entrepreneur and/or small business owner.

When I first started to incorporate various forms of speaking into my business, I went through an array of emotions before speaking. No matter how I felt, I just kept speaking, kept looking for opportunities to speak, and kept honing my message.

I knew I had something to share. I love with all my heart to see someone with a dream accomplish that dream with my assistance. That is my purpose and that is my calling in life. So, when I speak from that mindset, it is easier and more relatable.

Tip: This is what I shared with a recent coaching client of mine. I told them to think about their child and how when their child accomplishes a task, they want to share it with anyone who will listen. (This applies to any situation. Think about something that you are so excited about and want to share with everyone you know). Think about how you feel. You are excited, fearless, and you remember every single detail of what you want to share. You share the details in such a way that whomever is listening can really feel as though they were there, experience what you are describing.

It is the same with your business. If you really love what you do, it will show in what you have to say. Think about that when stepping onto a stage, being a guest on a radio show, or when speaking in front of people. You simply need to tap into what makes you excited and connected to what you want to share. The more connected you are to that very core, the more emotion will show up in how you speak.

For example, Charles Barkley is a very passionate and opinionated sports commentator. While you may not always believe in his delivery, you can tell he is very knowledgeable about his expertise in sports. When people see that, they will lean in and listen more. When people listen to you more, they are connecting with you. At that very point, what you share will absorb in a much stronger way.

Be Content Driven

Before you develop your content, you must ensure that what you are developing is in line with the issues your audience is facing and in line with your expertise. To establish your credibility in this, your audience must see that you are current on the issues facing them. Here are some suggestions on how you can assess what issues they are facing:

- Ask them. Attend the leadership teams of the organizations your audience belongs to and see if you can have the members take a survey.

- Ask providers that provide complimentary services to your audience what they have heard about the needs of your audience.

- Stay current. Read the magazines, blogs, and any industry publications to stay current on trends in your industry.

When developing your content, begin with the end in mind: ask yourself, *"What do I want my audience to do as a result of listening to me? What do I want them to walk away with?"*

For close to a decade, I ran and operated a professional speaker management agency. One of the most challenging skills for a speaker to learn is how to not sell from the stage. Gone are the days where you have to end every presentation with a sales pitch or make an offer. People want to hear high value content, step-by-step instructions, real life examples, and methods on how to implement what you shared. Focus on that and you will have people who want to use your services. You won't have to pitch them . . . your high value content will drive them to you.

On the other hand, you want to ensure the audience knows you have great programs, products, and services that are beneficial to them. So how do you marry the two?

Here are three super easy sales techniques you can use that are not "salesy" or inauthentic in any way:

- *Sow Seeds*—When sharing your presentation, integrate information about your programs without just coming out about your program. Drop authentic seeds about what you do and what you offer. The key is to make sure it fits with the content you are sharing. Make sure you are providing great content.

- *Be Straight*—Tell people up front that you'll give them as much as you can around the topic today, but then you'll share more on how they can take it farther at the end of your talk. This way they expect you to share an offer with them.

- *Provide Client Stories*—Share stories of clients and their successes or results throughout your talk, preferably to enhance the points you're discussing. Make sure to share not just a customer testimonial, but also their problem, why they came to you, briefly what you did with them, and then what the result was that the client achieved from doing that.

Be Results Based

Whether you are on the radio, giving a speech, or hosting your own teleseminar, fill your presentation with stories that show how your business has addressed problems and provided solutions for other clients. When you share stories to show rather than tell what it is you do, you simultaneously entertain, inform, and build an authentic trust within your audience.

> **Tip:** Keep in mind that your ideal clients need to feel like they know you, they want to like you and they need to trust you. This is what is known as the *Know-Like-Trust* Factor. They need to know you have helped others just like them. The more you demonstrate an authentic understanding of your ideal client's needs, the more believable it is to them that you and what you offer are the tools they have been looking for or need.

Your Action Task

What are three topics you can speak about as it relates to your business?

- With each topic you listed, write down three to five results-based content that someone would gain from hearing you?

- Since we want to stay in a spirit of authenticity, look at the topics you wrote and think about the clients who have had success with your services. You will want to share their success in your presentation.

- . Practice, practice, and practice. You need to ensure you know your presentation well. The last thing you want to do is be in front of your ideal clients and appear to not know your material well.

- Next, began to look for associations and groups where your ideal clients hang out. Those are the groups you want to get in front of to speak. Make a list of those groups, and make a commitment to contact at least three to five a day, either by email or phone.

Here is a quick tip if you are wondering *how* to reach out to a group to ask to speak. My advice is to keep it simple. Here are a couple of sample emails you can use when reaching out. Customize them to fit your personality.

Hello Carol,

My name is Denise Smith and I am a Leadership Development Consultant. I wanted to inquire as to how I may submit my information for your consideration to speak with your organization. I have followed the LEAD Group for some time and I truly enjoy the level of content your organization always delivers. I appreciate your time and consideration of my email. I look forward to hearing from you.

Or . . .

Hello Carol,

My name is Denise Smith and I am a Leadership Development Consultant, and my company is Lead R US (www.leadrus.com). I wanted to inquire as to how I may submit my information for your consideration to speak at your upcoming event. My expertise lies in leadership development, communication, and team building. I would like to invite you to visit my website where you can learn more about me, (provide website address). I appreciate your time and consideration of my request. I look forward to hearing from you.

Keep it simple and quick. The subject line should read: *Information Request.*

Below are twenty-two avenues by which you can infuse speaking into your business. This is truly the BEST way to reach your audience and build your business. You don't have to be a professional speaker to infuse speaking into your business. As you read the list below, keep in mind these are suggestions, and not all will fit your business. These are written to help spark ideas for you.

1. Contact local radio stations to be interviewed.

2. Contact national radio stations to be interviewed.

3. Contact online radio shows to be interviewed (BlogTalk Radio & Voice America).

4. Host your own radio show.

5. Speak at a four-year college campus (student activities, Greek life, human resources, new student orientation, residence life, career development etc.).

6. Speak at a two-year college campus.

7. Contact private colleges.

8. Speak for national conferences (keynotes, breakout sessions).

9. Speak for state conferences (keynote, breakout sessions).

10. Speak at training meetings (seek avenues in your industry where you can infuse training or gain training contracts).

11. Be the main speaker at a networking event (contact local or state/nationwide groups, depending on the scope of where you want to grow your business).

12. Host your own teleseminars.

13. Be a guest expert on a teleseminar.

14. Host your own webinar series.

15. Be a guest expert on a webinar series.

16. Host your own audio or video telesummit (this is where you assemble experts in your field who speak on different subjects your audience is drawn to).

17. Speak at retreats.

18. Host your own retreats.

19. Serve as a panel expert.

20. Be a facilitator at an event.

21. Host your own online TV show.

22. Seek out opportunities to be on an online TV show as a guest expert.

About Kimberly Pitts

Kimberly Pitts is both a Branding & Marketing Strategist and Developer. She is dedicated to helping entrepreneurial women use branding and marketing strategies to position their businesses in the market, attract their target audiences, create influential brands, realize more income, and enjoy freedom in both their businesses and their lives. She does this through her premier training-based mastermind program—Thrive Academy, her Branding VIP Program, the Packaged for Growth Annual Conference, and a myriad of ongoing training programs.

Anything but conventional, Kimberly is here to provide expert coaching and mentoring to better position you and your business for greater influence.

Learn More Here:
UImpact.net

Continue the Conversation on . . .

Facebook: Facebook.com/UImpact
Twitter: Twitter.com//Uimpact